Carla Muñoz Slaughter received law degrees from Harvard and Cambridge before spending several years in practice as a corporate lawyer. She then lectured in law at City University, the University of London and as adjunct professor at the University of Notre Dame in London. After her own children left home, she realised the dogs were not going to be able to do Kumon maths and so she also volunteered as a school governor and with other educational charities.

Her hobbies and interests include explaining things, feeding people, history and cross-country skiing. She loves dogs and ice cream, although not at the same time.

This is for all of the young people who have been part of my life.

Carla Muñoz Slaughter

TUPPENCE IN THE BANK

An Intelligent Beginner's
Guide to Investing

AUSTIN MACAULEY PUBLISHERS™
LONDON • CAMBRIDGE • NEW YORK • SHARJAH

Copyright © Carla Muñoz Slaughter 2023

The right of Carla Muñoz Slaughter to be identified as author of this work has been asserted by the author in accordance with sections 77 and 78 of the Copyright, Designs and Patents Act 1988.

All rights reserved. No part of this publication may be reproduced, stored in a retrieval system, or transmitted in any form or by any means, electronic, mechanical, photocopying, recording, or otherwise, without the prior permission of the publishers.

Any person who commits any unauthorised act in relation to this publication may be liable to criminal prosecution and civil claims for damages.

A CIP catalogue record for this title is available from the British Library.

ISBN 9781398497764 (Paperback)
ISBN 9781398497771 (ePub e-book)

www.austinmacauley.com

First Published 2023
Austin Macauley Publishers Ltd®
1 Canada Square
Canary Wharf
London
E14 5AA

Special thanks to Saskia Herz Mower and Rachel Dumbrell for encouraging me, to Lauren Johncock for sitting inside listening to the first outline on a sunny Sunday, and to Laura Riggall and Davide Locatelli for their invaluable skills in reading and helping me to edit the first draft. All errors, of course, remain my own.

Table of Contents

Preface	11
Chapter One: Introduction	19
Chapter Two: Savings Accounts, Other Investments, Shares, and Bonds	44
Chapter Three: Risk and Diversification	62
Chapter Four: Sources of Information and How to Invest	77
Chapter Five: ISAs, SIPPs and Taxes	99
Chapter Six: Borrowing Money and Home Ownership	115
Chapter Seven: The Other Stuff	127

Preface

There were several inspirations for this book; its purpose is to demystify how the stock market works, to discuss what types of investment options exist, consider the impact of different types of taxation and suggest ways to obtain information.

The first inspiration came from many years of teaching business associations and mergers to intelligent postgraduate law students. My goal was to ensure that the students could read the business section of a daily newspaper with some degree of understanding by the time they left the class. So, every time we met, we would go over the leading stories and discuss how they related to what we were studying. To my initial surprise, some of them would suddenly freeze and look horrified at the mention of interest rates or any other number (a bit the way older people do with technology). These were usually people who had been fine at maths in school until algebra was introduced, whereupon they became convinced that numeracy was not for them. I would try to convince the sceptical students (hopefully I succeeded) that financial literacy has relatively little to do with advanced numeracy. Algebra (not to mention what comes after it) really is a very boring subject; the good news is that most of life does not require it. Year five maths, a calculator and access to the internet are sufficient. It was an annual challenge, in the limited time available at the beginning of class, to persuade my students that most of what I was going to say was easy to understand and that none of it involved higher maths. For example, when interest rates go up, investing in shares is less attractive because shares are risky while saving in banks becomes more attractive because deposits are insured. Yes, there are complex financial instruments and derivatives but i) they are not suitable for retail investors and ii) arguably the people who deal in them, for all their mathematical brilliance, were responsible for the crash and great recession of 2008, so they aren't always a good idea. The stock market goes up and it goes down, often for geopolitical reasons rather than anything to do with a company's balance sheet. A company's earnings are better or worse than expected and it has an effect on the share price: note, "better" or "worse", no numbers needed. Yes, the numbers are important, but these days there are other people to do this work for you and the answers are easily available, for free, on the internet. It has been extremely gratifying, in recent years to have former students tell me that this section of the course (at least!) was useful to them in later life.

The second inspiration came from my own experience of being surrounded, in both my professional and private life, by people working in the financial services sector and being dissuaded by them from making or even trying to understand investment decisions because I was a lawyer and not a banker. Then, later, finding myself in a situation where I had to make those decisions and discovering that, while I made mistakes, professional money managers, although quick to use lots of jargon and be patronising, did not always do very well either. Moreover, they still expected to be paid fees even when they lost money for me. Lawyers are professionals and, like doctors, have fiduciary obligations to their clients. This means that they have always to put the interests of the client above their own financial or other benefit. People who sell you financial services have to tell the truth, but do not, in law, have fiduciary obligations to act in the client's best interests. They are perfectly entitled to encourage you to buy their service or product even when it is not preforming well compared to others. A company promoting its private pension would not point out that a given individual might be better off with an ISA, and so forth.

There were so many avoidable mistakes I made and so many things I wished someone had told me. I found other friends of my own generation in the same situation. Our parents had all had workplace pensions so we did not grow up hearing about the need to have a private pension. We came of age in a high interest rate environment when leaving money in a bank account to compound was a perfectly sensible plan. Investing seemed like a rather risky activity, so it seemed best to just put some money into a standard pension plan and forget about it, hoping for the best. All of the books on the subject were either full of economic theory and mathematical equations designed to teach would-be bankers or else about basic advice to avoid pay day loans. Different websites promoting different products contained a lot of information, but not all of it was disinterested and none of it was comprehensive.

To bring in a bit of the arts, there lived in the 17th century Spain, a famous poet called Luis de Gongora. His work was so difficult to understand that a phrase was coined: a "Gongorismo", to describe a "cultivated obscurity of style". According to the Encyclopaedia Britannica, Gongorismo involved a "taste for the construction of literary enigmas, puzzles, labyrinths, and visual designs, all presented in an esoteric, Latinate style, [which] led to cabalistic and occult exercises". All professions and service businesses have their own impenetrable jargon which are designed to confuse, intimidate, alarm and exclude outsiders; financial services are no exception.

"Gongorismos" convince the public that it is incapable of understanding or making investment decisions without professional certifications and calculus. This rather patronising belief is exacerbated by the culture of contempt towards anyone not hugely successful in the financial services sector. The many films which depict this culture are not exaggerating. *Wall Street*, *Barbarians at the Gate, The Wolf of Wall Street* and *The Big Short* may be out of date but still show a realistic depiction of the culture, despite the rise of governance concerns. There is a view that anyone not qualified to make a fortune in an investment bank is rather dim, not capable of managing any money at all, and should certainly not be querying the actions of those who manage money on their behalf. Fifty years ago, when there was no internet, this idea might have had some validity, but it is certainly not the case today with all of the information available on the internet, tracker funds, services to follow, and so forth (discussed below). Nowadays we can all have people to do the number crunching for us. The internet also makes it much easier to "free ride" on the opinions of multiple investment analysts.

My final inspiration came during the lockdowns of 2020 and 2021 when my university-age children, and their friends who lived with us during that period, were a satisfyingly captive audience at the dinner table as we observed the roller-coaster financial markets. I had the blissful experience of being able to do what every middle-aged person longs for: telling them what I wished I had known at their age. Bored by lockdown, I decided to consolidate this information and read my way through reams of information, and sit through endless financial webinars. Frustrated by not being able to teach, no one was safe from my attempts to explain things: the emergency builder fixing the roof even had a brief lecture explaining short selling (in fairness, he did ask). I then drafted in even more of my younger friends as I went through the first few outlines of what I thought needed explanation, asking them whether they found the information useful. They did, and this book is the result.

A caveat: the government regularly changes and amends taxes, student loans and savings schemes. The official budget takes place in the autumn, but recently major changes have also been announced in the spring statement and sometimes even at other times in between statements. The impact of tax changes can be enormous and it isn't usually good news. Markets rise and fall, as do interest rates, and new products and ways of investing are always being invented. Teaching law, I always felt that the ability to "issue spot" was the most important quality as a lawyer, as the actual answer could always be researched and the exams I gave reflected that approach. Consider what follows to be guidance on "issue spotting", rather than the answer. This is an introduction to the subject for the layperson; it is definitely not intended to be a how-to guide for prospective bankers or wealth managers. There is no need to read everything at once, dip in and out as needed and remember always to check the current state of the information.

Finally, my thanks to all of my sons' Sunday night supper guests who listened politely as I expounded; their questions and our discussions helped to frame the first draft of this book. I definitely owe them a few more dinners, free of any discussion of the stock markets, the effect of disruptive technology or proposed governance reforms.

Acknowledgements: Special thanks to Saskia Herz Mower and Rachel Dumbrell for encouraging me, to Lauren Johncock for sitting inside listening to the first outline on a sunny Sunday, and to Laura Riggall and Davide Locatelli for their invaluable skills in reading and helping me to edit the first draft. All errors, of course, remain my own.

Chapter One:
Introduction

History, as taught in many schools goes a bit like this: dinosaurs, cavemen, pharaohs, Greeks and Romans, knights in shining armour, Henry VIII, Victorians, the World Wars and...now. Here, then (with apologies for the over-simplification), is the (entirely optional but interesting) equivalent romp through the history of financial investing.

People save and invest for many reasons, whether for a house purchase, a rainy day, to provide for old age, to have an income after disability, or simply to lie on a beach somewhere consuming peeled grapes and mojitos. There are many kinds of investments, including property, which is probably the most common. Owners of property have considerable expenses (and time) to maintain the property and the risk to the owner's assets is unlimited if something goes wrong, although of course they may be insured. The market for property is also notoriously illiquid and it can be very difficult to sell if circumstances change and there is a need to raise cash. The advantage of investing in companies that are publicly traded on the stock exchange is the ability to:

i. dispense with the need to supervise and manage an enterprise; while
ii. still retaining ownership of the capital;
iii. in the hope that it will generate some form of return;
iv. through the efforts of others;
v. with both limited liability for the company's debts and the advantage of a liquid market (the stock exchange).

In such an enterprise, the employees and managers are compensated by salaries and the owners of the capital are compensated for the use of their funds by some form of return, whether capital growth or dividends. Ideally, dispensing with the need for close supervision also allows investors to diversify, so that they do not have all of their investment eggs in one basket. It is perfectly possible to be both an investor and a manager as the owner of a business but that requires a large degree of time, energy, and expertise, which may not always be possible, especially in later life. In early history, the property owner/investor-manager model was really all that was available, whether as a small business owner or a feudal overlord. There was no equivalent of today's diversified portfolio of shares in many different companies that are professionally managed by others.

The Middle Ages

As we all know, early civilisations were based on hunting and gradually moved on to agrarian societies with a form of barter and then, eventually, early money in the form of coins which had value in and of themselves. The value of a gold or silver coin was based on the scarcity and value of the coin itself, rather than being symbolic of any store of value. At this point in time, real value lay primarily in the ownership of land. Acquiring land was executed by methods that we would now consider morally dubious such as invading with an army, conquering (possibly murdering or enslaving) the residing population and taking their land. Or, if you were a small warlord, just hitting your neighbouring warlord over the head with a battle axe and proceeding in much the same way. You then hoped that no one would do the same to you and that your children would look after you in your old age before they inherited your land. This was a fairly standard method of asset management throughout the early

Middle Ages. Under the prevailing feudal system, nearly everyone had an assigned place in society: warriors and landowners were responsible to an overlord, and the king and clerics were responsible to the church. The church even had its own legal system; for centuries, any cleric who committed a crime was tried by the church in separate ecclesiastical courts. The peasants were responsible to the landowner, while the poorest peasants were serfs, tied to the land in a structure similar to slavery. The serfs were not allowed to leave the land and were subject to all sorts of other restrictions on their liberty. A serf had to do unpaid work for the landowner for a certain number of days a year and even ask for the landowner's permission before they could marry. The thought of any individual who was not contained and constrained in this hierarchy was considered dangerous and even contrary to the law of God.

The small number of people who lived in towns and were thus outside of this system could, therefore, not be left to their own devices to pursue anything as alarming as individual liberty. Royal charters were the solution that evolved. Larger towns could be granted royal charters by the king and, consequently became cities. Cities were responsible directly to the crown and were given a degree of rulemaking authority. They controlled their people through their own laws and hierarchical systems involving guilds that governed different trades and professions (many surviving examples of medieval guild houses still exist). The status of the City of London was confirmed by William the Conqueror, affirmed in the following century, and is still, today, technically the City of London Corporation. These royal charters, which gave legal personality to cities and universities, became in time the forerunners of the modern corporation. The size of these towns and their urban populations increased significantly after the bubonic plague swept through the country in the 14th century in a devastating global pandemic also known as the Black Death. The consequent reduction in the overall population led to a labour shortage that meant that serfs and peasants had greater power and were less inclined to stay on the land under the cosh of a feudal overlord. In 1381, there was even a peasant rebellion under the leadership of a man called Wat Tyler. The rebellion was ultimately unsuccessful, but it was the beginning of the end for the feudal system.

Of course, it was impractical for those who lived in cities to rely on land as a measure of value. Coins were issued by mints (authorised by the crown) in varying denominations, and were used to buy life's necessities, to trade and to save. In the absence of banks, savers had no option but to try to store their coins in a physically secure location, either at home or perhaps with a local goldsmith who had a strong room. So compared to today, saving was both inefficient and difficult and borrowing was even more so. Usury, or lending money at interest, was forbidden to Christians by church law. As non-Christians, Jews were permitted to lend money at interest but between the frequent horrific persecutions and eventual expulsion of the Jewish community by Edward I in 1290, this was not going to provide an adequate market for borrowers. If the lender cannot charge interest to compensate for the loss of the use of the funds and the risk that they might be lost, there isn't much incentive to lend money. This makes it harder to borrow money in order to start a new business. Saving is both less secure and less profitable if the saver cannot earn interest and must hide coins under the mattress where they might be stolen. This made saving for old age (for those who reached it) rather difficult, not to mention the possibility that you might live longer than expected and simply run out of the coins under the mattress. It was possible to invest some of the coins in a share of a business or perhaps, a ship, and hope for a share of the profits, but there were very few laws governing such arrangements and the risk was considerable.

In Europe, wealthy merchants in the Italian city-states, particularly the Venetians, were more active in early forms of banking and investment in overseas ventures, but there was relatively little such activity in England. There were no state or workplace pensions, although the guilds generally provided some charity to members who had fallen on hard times. For the exceptionally fortunate, the king might provide a pension or sinecure in the form of an income or rent for a royal property, but this was obviously not a universal solution. Finally, the childless might assign their property to a convent or monastery in return for care in the remaining years of their lives. This avenue was also open to those with children who had annoyed them.

The Age of Exploration, Early Capitalism, and the Industrial Revolution

The age of exploration in the 16th century heralded the beginning of change. Early voyages to the new world (think Christopher Columbus) were funded by the Spanish crown as explorers sought to reach the Far East by ship and break the Venetian monopoly on the spice trade. The Spaniards, upon reaching the new world, found that they had not reached the Maluku Islands in Eastern Indonesia (commonly referred to as the Spice

Islands due to their abundance of nutmeg, mace and cloves), but had instead found an even more valuable supply of silver and other commodities in Mexico and South America. The Spanish crown retained a monopoly on these ventures and, for a time, was regularly harassed by state-sponsored English pirates (including Sir Francis Drake) who did their best to relieve them of some of these treasures. In due course, explorers from England decided to set out on their own ventures, first to North America and then eventually to India and the Spice Islands. Voyages such as that of the Mayflower to what is now New England, were undertaken for religious or ideological reasons; others were for profit. For the more commercial ventures, it was essential to have enough money to buy and equip a ship or ships; this meant investors were needed. They also needed a charter to create an investment vehicle with a personality separate from that of its multiple owners.

Here, we come to the interesting bit: it wasn't legally permissible to put together a company with a separate legal personality without a charter from the crown. Without the royal charter, the investors would have simply been a large unwieldy partnership and it was essential for the enterprise to be separate from its investors to limit liability. Partners have unlimited liability because they conduct business in their own names; this means that if something goes wrong with the business, the partners stand to lose their personal assets. Thus, a partner would have needed to be highly involved with the business to monitor activity and keep track of the other partners. However, with an investment in a chartered company, the investors stood only to lose what they had put into the company, rather than everything they owned, allowing them to focus on other matters such as their own businesses. Investing small amounts in companies also allowed for diversification, which in turn reduced risk for the investor.

So, using the precedent of the royal charters granted to cities such as London, the crown granted new charters allowing companies to be formed. Importantly, the crown retained the monopoly to grant such charters, as it still does today. This led to the creation of widely known companies such as the Hudson Bay Trading Company for North America and the famous (or infamous) East India Trading Company, which at one point had its own private army. Soon, investors were able to buy shares in these ventures in the hope that the ships would come home laden with profitable goods, allowing the investors themselves to reside in London rather than taking dangerous trips across the high seas risking storms, enemies, pirates, and scurvy.

At the same time, other businesses began to copy the idea of selling shares, sometimes without the benefit of a charter or any other kind of regulation. They weren't supposed to do this, but there was no mechanism to enforce the law. These shares were famously traded in the coffee houses of London, the precursor to today's Stock Exchange. Of course, it didn't always work out and fortunes were lost as well as made. Famously, the physicist Isaac Newton lost a fortune in a market bubble involving the South Sea Company when the market crashed in 1720 (which just goes to show that being quantitative isn't everything). Part of the problem was that several overvalued and unchartered companies had been formed as "get rich quick" schemes. The government responded by passing the first company law legislation: the Bubble Act of 1720. The Act reiterated that no one was permitted to form a company without a royal charter, confirming the government monopoly on company formation. The collapse of the South Sea Bubble caused enormous losses and even bank failures, but with the profits to be made from emerging markets in the new world, the stock market continued to grow.

The investment model proved to be popular and soon expanded to include the heinous slave trade and the related triangular trade in sugar and cotton with North America. The South Sea Company itself had been formed in part to supply slaves to Latin America. The reason why so many modern institutions and historical figures are now being taxed with a historical involvement in slavery is simply that taking a share in a slave ship was a very common (and profitable) form of investment, particularly in the west of England in places such as Bristol. The dreadful Royal African Company is another case in point. Established in 1660 by the Stuart kings together with London merchants, it initially traded gold and eventually became one of the most significant companies in the West African slave trade. Enormous fortunes could be and were made in the slave trade. As slavery was illegal in England itself (although not in the colonies of the British Empire) and the consequences were not immediately visible, people hoping not to miss out on these profits may have been able to distance themselves emotionally from the appalling reality, although there were others who campaigned against it from the outset and even renounced sugar on the grounds that it was the product of slavery. Thankfully, the slave trade was outlawed in 1807 and abolished throughout the Empire in 1833, although slave owners in the colonies were compensated. For an interesting, albeit fictional, exploration of the British slave trade and the attempt at "emotional distancing", read Barry Unsworth's novel *Sacred Hunger*.

The industrial revolution soon provided another source of investment. Unlike traditional artisanal shops, factories with heavy machinery needed large amounts of capital investment, creating very profitable opportunities for investors. The new railways also required much larger sums than one individual could provide. The opportunities for investment in these new technologies meant that more and more companies were being created, mostly without any regulation. The Joint Stock Companies Act of 1844 made it possible for businesses to incorporate officially. This was followed by the Limited Liability Act of 1855, which made it clear that shareholders were not personally liable for the company's debts and only stood to lose the investment they had made. There was still relatively little "truth in advertising" for those seeking to invest in such new companies, and promotors often made extravagant and unjustifiable claims about new companies. Insider dealing was both widespread and completely legal; there also was a certain amount of outright fraud. Fortunes were made but also lost. However, as the saying goes, "a rising tide lifts all boats" and the 19th century was a time of enormous technological, economic, and even geographic expansion. This was particularly true in the United States (U.S.) and, for a time, wealthy Americans became the oligarchs of the western world. The entire plot of the television soap opera *Downton Abbey* revolves around the fact that the English aristocracy continued to disapprove of trade and instead put their faith in land ownership. As a result, they were somewhat late to the party and developed a habit of marrying wealthy American heiresses to compensate for the failure to invest in industry at an earlier date.

The Roaring Twenties

By the time of the First World War in 1914, stock markets and exchanges were well established and the crown or state monopoly on issuing charters was well accepted. Anyone with a reasonable amount of money to invest would hope to invest at least some of the money in the stock market. Ideally, families would want to leave the capital untouched for the next generation to inherit and to allow them to live off the income on the capital, although death duties made this increasingly difficult in later years. There was still almost no regulation of the veracity of the claims made by those seeking capital, but following the war, the rising tide continued to lift most of the boats most of the time. In fact, many people made enormous fortunes and more and more people who were inexperienced investors plunged into the market, afraid of missing the boat (to continue the maritime metaphor).

There is a story, perhaps apocryphal, that in 1929 the American millionaire John D. Rockefeller realised that the market was turning into a bubble and sold many of his shares when a young man shining his shoes advised him to get in on investing. (There are shades of this story in the film, *The Big Short*, when the protagonists realise that lap dancers who cannot meet their payments are trying to hold down mortgages on two properties). In the 1920s, the increasing bubble was complicated by two factors. First, the use of "margin" or debt to buy shares. People borrowed money to invest in the stock market and offered the shares they bought as security for the loan. When the bubble burst and the stock market fell, the shares also fell in value and the bank had less collateral. This meant that the bank might "call" the loan and demand immediate repayment which the borrower would then be unable to make unless they sold other assets, driving prices down still further. In some cases, it was impossible to repay the loan and the borrower had no alternative but bankruptcy, or in some cases, even suicide. If the borrower was an employer, the employees then lost their jobs and so forth. To complicate matters further still, savers were concerned about the stability and solvency of banks leading to "runs", where the bank door was closed as it was impossible to meet the demands of all those who wanted to withdraw their savings. There is a good example of this in the original *Mary Poppins*, where the children cause a panicked run on their father's bank. *Mary Poppins* also has the ultimate song about compound interest "*Tuppence in the Bank*", (quoted at the beginning of the book) if anyone would care to revisit a childhood favourite.

The second complication was the almost complete lack of any kind of "truth in advertising" legislation in the stock market. This was somewhat less of a problem in the London markets where the "old boys' club" created a degree of self-regulation. Anyone who behaved too badly would find that he was ostracised or "shunned and avoided". However, the expanding economies of the American and other overseas markets were another matter entirely. Under the U.S. Constitution, the federal government only has the power to make laws in the areas where authority has been expressly granted, such as foreign policy. There is nothing in the constitution granting any power for the federal government to regulate stock markets or indeed any aspect of company law. As we will see later, they eventually found a way around this, but in 1929, chaos reigned. Each separate state had its own separate laws on company formation and the sale of shares, without any standardised disclosure requirements. Even within the states, there was very little enforcement of such laws as did exist. Given the state of technology at the time, it was very difficult for an investor in New York or London to gain an accurate picture of what was going on in a company in Illinois, Texas, or California. This was fine so long as most of the investments turned out well most of the time. It was only when the music stopped in the crash of 1929 that the chaos became apparent.

Regulation up to Today, the Importance of the American Market, and Thermogenic Ice Cream

The crash of 1929 was a disaster and the ensuing Great Depression of the 1930s led to considerable hardship. Not only did the stock market crash, but there were also bank failures that meant that many people lost their savings. Bank deposits are insured today but that was not the case at the time. It might seem that only wealthy families would have been affected but the bankruptcies and loss of demand created a domino effect, which reached everyone. The effect was less marked in the United Kingdom (U.K.), but in the U.S. it was catastrophic and, of course, the British public and banks were also invested in the U.S. market, partly because of the opportunities to be found in an emerging market and partly because of its sheer size. The government of President Franklin Roosevelt, elected in 1932, was desperate for a solution. Under his guidance, legislators created a programme of public works called the "New Deal" in an effort to kick-start the economy. This was somewhat successful, although there are those who argue that it was the Second World War that finally pulled the country out of the depression. In fact, it took 25 years for the market to reach the highs of 1929 again Fig. 1).

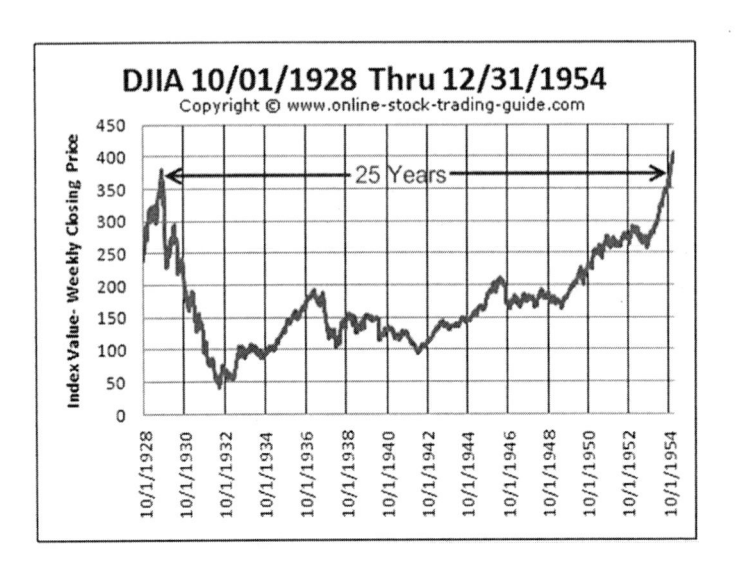

Figure 1. The crash of 1929 and the ensuing Great Depression. By 1954, the market recovered to the weekly closing price highs of 1929 after a 25-year period.

There remained the problem of what to do with the financial markets. The financial markets are essential, not only for investors, but for companies and job creation. To simplify greatly, if someone has a brilliant idea but no money, that person can raise capital in the financial markets, build the factory (or whatever infrastructure is needed), create lots of new jobs and supply us all with a wonderful new product. This is obviously good for the economy as a whole, not just for investors who receive a good return as a reward for risking their capital and investing in the brilliant new idea. For example, take a personal favourite hypothetical investment, beloved by generations of students: the Thermogenic Ice Cream Company. Drinking cold water burns calories and ice cream is cold. If an inventor were to find a way to make ice cream that actually burned calories because it was cold, this would surely increase the sum total of human happiness in addition to making a great deal of money for those who had invested in the company. (The ice cream would be organic and fair trade of course). As the company would be enormously successful, it would also create jobs. Moreover, the company would pay tax on its profits, the investors would pay tax on the dividends and the employees would pay tax on their salaries. The economy benefits and everyone is better off, especially, in this case, the consumer.

When people deposit money in a savings bank, the bank is then able to loan that money to businesses or people who want to buy homes. The borrowers pay interest on the loan, the bank takes a cut, and some of the interest is passed to the savers in the form of interest on their savings. For companies, raising money in the stock market can be an attractive alternative to borrowing money from a bank because (i) banks don't usually want to take the risk of lending the enormous sums that can be raised by selling shares, (ii) bank loan agreements can be extremely restrictive, and (iii) lenders may ask for personal guarantees from the owners of new businesses. Most non-communist governments want to encourage people to save and invest in order for them to make financial provision for themselves in their old age, and so forth. For investors and savers to take their money out from under the mattress, they need to have confidence both in banks and in the financial markets.

It is fair to say that by the early 1930s there was very little confidence in the U.S. market, at least among rational people. The American government needed a way to address this problem and overcome the absence of authority for federal regulation. The answer could be found in another part of the constitution: a bit called the "commerce clause". This clause gave the federal government the authority to regulate interstate commerce, that is, commercial activity between and among the many states. Large scale trade in publicly held shares (those traded on a stock exchange) obviously involved crossing state lines and involved the "means and instrumentality" of interstate commerce: the postal service, the telephone, telegrams and so forth.

Using the commerce clause to give it authority, the U.S. government embarked on a comprehensive scheme of regulation for publicly traded companies. Internal, intrastate matters such as the election of directors, declaration of dividends and directors' duties to the company were to continue to be (and still are) regulated by the individual states. The federal regulation was based on a series of disclosure requirements in documents to be filed with regulatory authority: the Securities and Exchange Commission (SEC). These come into play when the company issues shares (whether for the first time or subsequently to raise additional capital) and when the company reports to the market and its shareholders. The essence of these requirements is truth; there must be no material misstatements or omissions. There is a template for each of the documents to be filed but it is not exclusive, and the company is required to disclose anything that a reasonable investor would consider relevant or "material". If the company fails to do so, it can be not only sanctioned by the SEC but also sued by investors. In the case of deliberate misstatements, there may also be criminal penalties. The SEC is, and is meant to be, scary.

Needless to say, the system hasn't always worked and there have been high-profile fraud cases such as the fall of Enron and the Madoff Ponzi scheme. There have also been terrible market crashes such as the sub-prime crisis in 2008, with the most recent being in March 2020. Many shares soared in value in the year following the pandemic, especially the technology shares which benefitted from lockdown and the trend towards home working. Unfortunately for investors, the market recovery was followed shortly thereafter by the fall in the value of shares triggered by the horrific and brutal invasion of Ukraine in 2022. Although no one can blame bankers and financial regulators for Covid-19 or the actions of a deranged Russian leader, they were clearly responsible for the crash of 2008 and the recession that followed. The SEC has a degree of rule-making authority and has tried to adjust the law following some of the more public scandals; it is also easily the most powerful securities regulation authority in the world. The U.S. laws and system are relevant to investors in other jurisdictions not only because some of the laws are extra-territorial but simply because the U.S. is the world's single largest capital market. In 2020, the market capitalisation of a single U.S. company, Apple, Inc., exceeded that of the leading U.K. share index, the FTSE 100. Moreover, the U.S. also contains many, if not most, of the clearing banks needed by banks in other countries. This meant, for example, that the U.S. authorities were able to apply pressure to bring an end to much of Swiss banking secrecy, simply because of concerns about insider dealing in the U.S., and more recently, to enforce some of the sanctions imposed on Russia following the invasion of Ukraine. The effect of U.S. securities laws is felt worldwide, a fact that is not always welcomed by other jurisdictions. Nonetheless, it means American markets and American law cannot be entirely disregarded by any serious investor.

In contrast, other jurisdictions and the London market were somewhat slower to adopt strict laws. Having tried various options, the U.K. now has its own law with obligations and civil and criminal penalties: the Financial Services and Markets Act 2000; and its own enforcement authority: the Financial Conduct Authority (FCA). The FCA has a great deal of authority to investigate misdeeds but does not yet inspire the same degree of terror as the SEC, although it may yet become more terrifying in the fullness of time.

In summary, regarding the overall effect of limited liability, these various schemes of securities regulation and bank insurance have had the desired effect of tempting large numbers of people and institutions to take their money out from under the mattress to put it back into banks and investment markets. Regulation today is an ever-increasing challenge with the use of the internet and the rise of cryptocurrencies; nonetheless, for those who choose to invest more conservatively (or perhaps sensibly), the shelter of financial regulation provides considerable protection compared to any other time in history.

Additional Reading

If anyone has been truly riveted by the extremely brief account of financial history above, and wishes to pursue further reading, here are some suggestions:

1. *Power and Profit: The Merchant in Medieval Europe*, Peter Spufford (2002)
2. *The Smartest Guys in the Room: The Amazing Rise and Scandalous Fall of Enron*, Peter Elkind (2004)
3. *The Ascent of Money: A Financial History of the World*, Niall Ferguson (2008). (Note: Also available as a television documentary)
4. *The Corporation That Changed the World: How the East India Company Shaped the Modern Multinational*, Nick Robbins (2012)
5. *Nathaniel's Nutmeg: How One Man's Courage Changed the Course of History*, Giles Milton (2012)

6. *The Anarchy: The Relentless Rise of the East India Company*, William Dalrymple (2020)

Chapter Two:
Savings Accounts, Other Investments, Shares, and Bonds

Why to Save and Save Early

The earlier in life you begin to save, the harder the money will work for you because of what has been called the "magic of compound interest". Compounding means letting the interest on savings earned each year stay in the account so that every year the amount of money on which interest is earned increases. The stock market equivalent is to invest in growth shares or to stay invested without taking profits and reinvesting any dividends.

The following excerpt from an article published on USnews.com gives a good example of using historical stock market performance as an indicator. So, investing even

small amounts at an early age can add up to a significant sum later.

> "The stock market is kindest to those who stay faithful to it longest. To see this, consider investors Jack, Jill, and Joey.
>
> Jack starts investing $200 per month when he's 25. By age 65, his portfolio is worth more than $520,000.
>
> Jill doesn't start investing until age 35. She also contributes $200 per month, but by 65, her portfolio is only worth about $245,000. By waiting ten years to start, she ends up with less than half what Jack accumulates.
>
> Joey, the late bloomer, starts investing $200 per month when he's 45 and after 20 years has only $100,000."

Bank Accounts

For most people, the first encounter with saving is the childhood piggy bank which functions along the lines of the medieval "coins under the mattress" investment model. Money is saved, but there is no return on the money and the value of the savings will be eroded by inflation if it isn't instead spent on sweets. From there, we may go on to "tuppence in the bank" with a first bank account. Putting money in the bank where it will earn interest and then allowing the interest to be compounded over time was for many years the gold standard conservative investment strategy. (Calculating compound interest may or may not be a difficult mathematical calculation, but it really doesn't matter because there are free compound inflation calculators on the internet – just look it up.).

Example one: In the 1980s it was possible to earn up to 15% per annum in a bank account. So, at 15% interest, if you invest £10,000, at the end of one year you would have £11,607.55. At the end of 10 years, letting the interest compound (without making additional deposits or taking any withdrawals) you would have £44,402.13. Magic.

Example two: The problem is that if interest rates are 1%, then, even letting the interest compound, you would only have £11,607.25 after 10 years.

Bank deposits are insured, at the time of writing up to £85,000 per account in the U.K. and somewhat more in the U.S. So, in a high interest rate environment, a savings account is a low-risk way to earn a good return on savings. There will never be the sort of exponential growth that is sometimes seen with new companies in the stock market, but those tend to be higher risk investments. If interest rates are high, cash is a good place to be for someone with a low appetite for risk. However, cash does not provide a good return when interest rates are low, let alone the historical lows they have reached at the time of writing. The other problem with cash is inflation. If inflation is running at 3% or 4% and interest rates are only 1-2% (which is where we are at the, again, time of writing), then the money sitting in a bank account becomes steadily less valuable over time as its value erodes. At 5% inflation, a cash deposit would devalue by 50% in just under 15 years. For someone very elderly, or who needs money in the immediate future, it may not be a problem, but it is a disastrous scenario for someone young who is looking to save for the long-term future. Moreover, the higher rate interest savings accounts are not instant access, they tend to be for a period of at least a year, during which time the money cannot be accessed without losing part or all of the interest. This means that part of the advantage of holding cash is lost.

One of the current problems with cash has arisen because savers in their 50s and 60s (who are now close to retirement) anticipated that the high interests of their youth would continue. Rates then fell dramatically, with catastrophic effects for those who put their retirement savings in cash. Someone who was young in the late 1980s planning to save £2 million into a bank account might have envisaged a luxurious private pension of £200,000 a year – 10% of £2 million. Unfortunately, that person, now nearing retirement age, is looking at 2% (at best) which is £40,000 a year – a very different lifestyle.

Despite the disadvantages of holding cash in a low interest rate/high inflation environment, financial advisors universally agree that several months' outgoings should be held in cash in case of emergencies, stock market corrections and unemployment. This amount obviously depends on individual circumstances and financial commitments. For the most part, you still must pay your bills and mortgage even if the sky has fallen. The one exception is student loans in the U.K. upon which payments do not need to be made during periods of unemployment.

OTHER FORMS OF SAVING: PROPERTY AND WORKPLACE PENSIONS

Of course, there are many ways to save and invest. These are detailed below.

Home Ownership

Buying a home is a form of investment while also providing a place to live. Home ownership is expensive, even after the deposit. Not only is there a mortgage to pay but also maintenance, insurance, the replacement of appliances and boilers, other bills and so forth. The advantage is that gains made on the sale of a primary residence are not currently taxed in the UK (although they are in the U.S.). However, nothing is ever entirely free, and homeowners also pay stamp duty upon purchase; this is even higher for rental properties or second homes. For aspiring landlords, profits on sale of a rental property are taxed as capital gains, although expenses incurred in renovating or maintaining the property can be deducted.

For many older people, a home is a nest egg that can be sold when they downsize in retirement. A smaller house with a nice lump of cash to get through retirement is a common financial goal of home ownership. Unfortunately, home ownership is now beyond the reach of many young people. Even for those who can afford a home, property is not a very liquid investment. The housing market goes down as well as up and it can be very difficult to sell at profit unless you are able to take a long-term approach. Most people borrow to buy a home and need to take out a mortgage. This means that if the housing market falls and the borrower needs to sell quickly and at a loss, they can be left owing the bank money for a property they no longer own. This is called "negative equity" and it is not a nice place to be.

Pensions

The term "pension" has a particular legal meaning distinct from ordinary savings. "Pensions" are regulated by the government and there are particular tax laws that apply which are different from the treatment of ordinary savings, like a bank account. For the fortunate few, there are workplace pensions. Private pensions not related to employment (self-invested personal pensions [SIPPs] and individual savings accounts [ISAs]) will be covered in more detail in *Chapter Five*.

There used to be (mostly for people aged over 70 now) a wonderful thing called a defined benefit or final salary scheme pension. In a defined benefit scheme pension, the employer guaranteed a pension to the employee, based on either their final or average salary, regardless of how the stock market or economy as a whole was doing. These pensions were not funded by the current earnings of the company but rather by investing the employer and employee contributions in the stock market and by making other investments. If the investments did well, everyone was happy, but if they did badly, it wasn't the employees' problem and the employer had to make up the shortfall. The lucky defined benefit scheme pensioners were able to relax as the money rolled in, month after month, thinking about the next cruise and ignoring the state of the stock market. £100,000 a year in the public sector may not seem like an enormous salary compared to earnings in the financial services sector, but it would be a lovely pension if you were given something approaching that amount, based on your final salary. At current rates, you would have to save £10 million to guarantee that retirement income by investing in a bank account or securing high grade government bonds (assuming no capital was taken). A civil service career is worth a lot more when the pension entitlement is considered.

Sadly, for today's workers, there are few such schemes left. Most company pensions are now based on a combination of employee and employer contributions with no guaranteed outcome. Even the public sector is moving towards this model, although, not surprisingly, with considerable resistance from unions. Most employees no longer have the luxury of ignoring the issue of their pensions, safe in the knowledge that the employer will deal with it. Many companies will offer a choice of pension funds and while choice is generally a good thing, employees may not always be equipped to make these choices. For those who have chosen to become financially literate, more choice is clearly preferable; even then, it means a lot more work and research. Under the recent auto-enrolment legislation, all employers must now offer employees the option of a pension to which the employee also contributes. The minimum contribution from the employers is 3% of the employee's annual salary. To take advantage of the scheme, employees must contribute 4%, which is effectively 5% with the government tax break. It is optional for employees to enrol in the scheme, although most people would not want to miss out on employer contributions.

Workplace pensions have other positive advantages, despite the loss of the final salary scheme. Pension contributions will be taken from the salary before tax, so that employee pays tax and National Insurance (NI) on a lower amount. With a SIPP (self-invested private pension) the amount is taken out after tax and then "grossed up" by the government, so that there is a similar income tax break. Moreover, workplace pension contributions have the added advantage of reducing the contributor's NI tax and possibly income tax band. Reducing the overall amount of taxable income means paying less NI, lower student loan repayments, possibly keeping means-tested child benefit and so forth.

Some companies will even allow employees to increase pension contributions through "salary sacrifice"; this can be very useful for someone on the cusp of losing benefits or paying more tax. The downside is that the amount saved cannot be accessed until the age of 55, so money saved in a pension of any kind is not available as a nest egg for other purposes. Because of the tax breaks, there are also limits to the amount that can be contributed each year (currently £40,000 a year or 100% of salary, whichever is lower) and a lifetime limit for total value, currently just over £1 million. Note that that is for the total value of all the individual's pensions. If £600,000 is invested well, it could easily grow to over £1 million. Anyone fortunate enough to have pensions approaching that mark would be well advised to consult an accountant or tax lawyer about next steps. Note, these rules change all the time so it is essential to check the up-to-date legislation.

NI also entitles those who have paid to receive a state pension, although the age of eligibility keeps increasing. Currently it is 67, rising to 68 for younger people. To receive the full state pension, you need to have worked for 35 years; even then, it only comes to about £9,300 a year, which is well below the poverty level. For those who have worked for less time the amount is pro-rated. So, all in all, not a great retirement plan for a prosperous (or even merely solvent) retirement.

Finally, because of the tax benefits associated with pension contributions, amounts received as pension in later life are taxed as ordinary income, even though it may seem that you are just taking back out money that you have saved. If you are a higher rate taxpayer, then you will be taxed at a higher rate. There is an exception: 25% may be taken out tax free upon reaching the age of 55; however, thereafter it is taxed. For someone who expects to be a higher rate taxpayer in retirement (whether through inheritance or general prosperity), it is worth hiring an accountant to help work through whether you would be better off prioritising investment in a tax-free ISA over pension contributions. On the other hand, there are currently inheritance tax advantages to investing in pensions, although this is probably not a priority for most people as they are setting out in life.

Pension schemes are heavily regulated, but they are not insured. They also make their money by charging fees, whether they do well or not. There is also no guarantee of good performance, as outcomes are at the mercy of the investment decisions made by the fund managers and results vary widely. Anyone investing in a workplace pension would be well advised to ask how well the fund performs relative to competitors and indeed, to the market as a whole. For a small employer, setting up an auto-enrolment scheme is a new and irritating administrative hassle, and it is entirely possible that not a lot of thought or research will have gone into the choice of scheme.

The Stock Market: Stocks (Shares) And Bonds

Savers invest in the stock market because it is a liquid investment that has significantly outperformed other areas over time. Without getting into exotic financial instruments, the stock market can be described as consisting of stock or shares (the same thing), and bonds. The Dow Jones industrial average, from 1900 to the present day, is shown in Fig. 2.

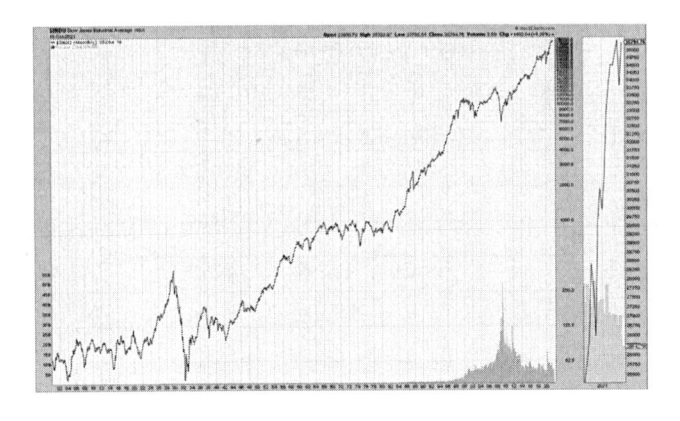

Figure 2.: The Dow Jones industrial average, from 1900-present. Stock charts can be accessed here.

Bonds: Bonds are a loan to a company, from investors, divided into small denominations. It is a loan, not a share in the business, which means that countries as well as firms issue bonds. If a company wants to borrow £1 million, it could issue one million bonds worth £1 each. That £1 is called the face or par value. The bonds would also have a term, just like a bank loan, for example for ten years. At the end of the ten years, each bondholder would get back the £1 per bond. In the interim, the company would pay interest and the bondholder would receive that interest as income, monthly, quarterly, or annually as specified. The interest rate paid would depend on the prevailing rate of interest at the time the bond was issued and the company's own creditworthiness. Riskier companies would pay a higher rate of interest to compensate for the risk. Bonds are attractive because they provide an almost guaranteed fixed income based on the stated interest rate. The income is "almost" guaranteed because, unlike the case with dividends, companies don't have to make a profit to pay their bondholders; interest is considered to be a cost of doing business and is even tax deductible from profits. Bondholders also have the advantage of "liquidation preference"; this means that if the company goes bankrupt, the bondholders get their money back before the shareholders.

Like shares, bonds are publicly traded on the stock exchange. The face value of the bond is fixed but the trading price of the bond will vary according to other interests as well as news about the company's or country's solvency. So, if interest rates are at 1% and someone has a 50-year bond left from the 1980s with a face value of £10 and a 15% coupon, that bond will trade for much more that £10 on the stock exchange unless, of course, the company is in danger of insolvency. At the time of writing, some of the highest yield bonds are available from unstable sovereign nations which are at risk of default. The risk is even higher because no one is going to invade a sovereign state with bankruptcy experts and sell off the assets to pay the creditors. So, they must pay a much higher rate of interest in order to be able to borrow.

For many years, savers were advised to increase substantially the percentage of bonds in a portfolio with age until it was nearly all in bonds by retirement. Someone who has stopped working needs a guaranteed income and cannot afford to take the risk of losing the capital investment. Bonds do not increase in value because the bondholders never get back more than the face amount, even if the company does well. This means inflation is a problem if the bond is not paying more than the rate of inflation. Investing in bonds will also not increase the value of your portfolio, something which is essential for younger investors. However, to put it bluntly, if you don't have that much longer to live, it isn't going to be a problem. Unfortunately for this investment thesis, we are all living much longer and may face 30 or even 40 years in retirement, rather than ten or twelve. To make matters worse, in a low interest rate environment, bonds just don't deliver the income they once did.

Shares: Shares are in essence a fractional interest in a company. This doesn't mean that each shareholder has a fraction of each desk, chair, and machinery, but rather, an interest in the legal entity that is the company. Companies can be either public or private. Private companies are owned by a limited number of shareholders and are not traded on a stock exchange. Shares in private companies can be very profitable, but the disadvantage is that there is no market for the shares. This means it is difficult to know the value of the shares at any one time and even more difficult to sell them if there is a disagreement or if money is needed. Moreover, many private companies have provisions making it impossible to sell the shares without the consent of the other shareholders.

What all companies have in common is:

1. **Separate legal personality**. The company is a separate person in law apart from the human beings connected with it.

2. **Limited liability**. This means the shareholders are not liable for the company's debts. Even if they have been earning large dividends for years, the shareholders are not liable if the company does something dreadful such as create an environmental disaster (like an oil spill). This is because of:

3. **Centralised Management**. The board of directors manages the company. Shareholders elect the directors and have limited rights to be consulted but directors make all operational decisions. In small companies, directors and

shareholders may be the same people but they must be careful to wear different "hats" depending on which role they are carrying out. In public companies, most shareholders never even meet the directors.

4. **Transferability of shares**. Unlike a partnership, the shareholders do not own the underlying assets of the company but shares in the company itself. This means it is much easier to transfer ownership of the shares.

5. **Immortality**. Shareholders are human and live and die but a company can go on forever, so long as it remains solvent.

Public Companies: In contrast to private companies, shares in public companies are bought and sold on the stock exchange daily. Companies choose to "list" their shares on a stock market because they want to raise money. In some cases, private companies "go public" to cash in on the value of a successful business. More frequently, the company needs money whether for a new idea, to expand, or for an acquisition. There is always the option to take a bank loan, but banks do not like to lend enormous sums of money and bank loan agreements can be very restrictive. Besides, bank loan interest payments must be made no matter how badly the company is doing. When a company raises equity capital by issuing shares, the shareholders share in both the risks and the rewards of the venture. There is no obligation for the company to pay dividends and little recourse if the shares do not rise in value (except in the case of fraud).

Indeed, many companies have a policy not to pay dividends, pursuing a higher share price instead. Shareholders are attracted by the hope that the shares will go up in value and/or that there will be a stream of dividend income. It is up to the directors to decide whether to declare a dividend, based on profits or choose to reinvest the money in the company. The company must live up to the statements of intent made in the disclosure documents that accompany the initial issue of shares, but after that the directors have considerable discretion. When a shareholder buys shares on the stock exchange they are buying from another shareholder, rather than the company itself. In this case, the buyer will have to rely on the company's annual filings for information. In reality, it is more likely to be the financial press or an investment advisor.

Chapter Three:
Risk and Diversification

Risk Factors for Share Prices

The value of the shares is determined in part by the underlying value and cash flows of the company, in part by how well it is doing compared to competitors, and in part (sometimes almost entirely) by "market sentiment". If something dreadful has just happened, the market will drop, sometimes very irrationally. Recent examples include the week after the tragic 9/11 attacks on the World Trade Center (temporary dip); the sub-prime mortgage crises in 2008 which led to the Great Recession (quite a long dip); and, of course, the recent Covid-19 pandemic. In February 2020, the stock market began to fall because of concerns about the pandemic. At one point in March, the stock market fell by 26% in four days. Some shares fell more than others, but nearly everything was down, except for companies that made bleach and hand sanitiser. Shares of Amazon fell from around $2000 to just under $1700. Amazon was clearly going to be a beneficiary of the lockdown crisis and was actively *hiring people*. It made sense that the shares of airlines, purveyors of workplace sandwiches and oil companies dropped. It made no sense at all for shares in-home delivery companies to go down. Amazon shares then rose to over $3000 a share in the next few months (although the shares have been more volatile since then). Lots of movement in share prices is called volatility and it can be very unnerving for investors. Investment platforms will tell you that overall drops of 10% are to be expected in any one year, but it is still stomach-churning when it happens.

Interest Rates: Interest rates are set by central banks as a tool, both to manage the economy and as part of monetary policy. So long as interest rates are low, investors looking for reasonable returns don't have many alternatives to the stock market. Investors are more reluctant to invest in the risk of the stock market when high bank interest rates offer a risk-free return. It is also more difficult for companies to raise capital in a high interest rate environment. Bank loans become more expensive, and shareholders also expect better returns, whether through dividends or growth. Individual borrowers and homeowners must pay more interest on loans and mortgages, and so have less disposable income to spend on goods and services. So, when interest rates go up, it doesn't tend to be good news for share prices.

Currency Fluctuations: Anyone who invests in a company based outside of their home jurisdiction takes the risk that the investment will go down in value if the currency in which the shares are denominated declines against the pound sterling. Less obviously, a U.K. based company that imports or exports will also be affected by exchange rate volatility.

Geopolitics: Just as the pandemic began to settle down and it seemed safe to go back into the water, Russia decided to invade Ukraine It goes without saying that this was obviously, first and foremost, a tragedy for the Ukrainian people. The markets crashed. This is the bubble above the head of an investor: *much of Europe depends on Russian gas (along with other commodities) and much of the world depends on Ukraine wheat. What if the gas is turned off? What if there is famine? What if prices rise so much there are riots? We could be vaporised; how do we price in the risk of nuclear war? Worse, a left-wing government might be elected. If that wasn't enough to worry about, is this going to give China ideas about invading Taiwan? Should we distance ourselves from China,* *upon which we are now very dependent, given the size of the market? Is this a new cold war? Look at the price of petrol! Should I buy shares in an oil company? They crashed during lockdown but are now back up! Etcetera....*

Very few companies were able to ride this out without a fall in the share price. Interestingly, the energy companies that did very badly during the pandemic rose sharply if they had access to non-Russian energy supplies. The shares of some small North Sea oil producers doubled in a few weeks.

Known and Unknown Unknowns: Company share prices will also fluctuate on a monthly or quarterly basis and when companies release reports on earnings, expected earnings and other developments. If a company releases wonderful earnings, greatly improved from the last quarter but still not what was anticipated, the share price may fall following the announcement. Companies that pay large dividends will normally see a slight drop once the dividend record date is announced. The large volume of share trading means that it is impractical to pay a dividend to the person who owns the shares on the day the dividend is actually paid. The solution is to declare a "record date"; shareholders of record on that date get paid the dividend. Anyone who buys after that date is out of luck until the next quarter.

Individual companies may experience disasters or triumphs which affect the share price. There are many examples of disasters, from oil spills to actual fraud. Some of the disasters, like being discovered to be employing illegal child labour, are entirely avoidable and may lead to litigation against those in charge. The triumphs include technological or medical breakthroughs and discoveries of new resources. Then there are known risk factors, like doing business in a country with an unstable political regime or being in an industry that is weather dependent. The unknown unknowns are trickier: terrible tragedies like 9/11 in the U.S. and the disaster of the Covid-19 pandemic. The pandemic was not something that individual businesses could have hedged for, but it was not a complete unknown and it is both surprising and disappointing that governments were not better prepared.

Just to be cheerful, there are five partly known unknowns that would be catastrophic for the worldwide economy and stock markets everywhere: an asteroid from outer space; a solar flare or natural disaster of immense magnitude; another pandemic, this time with a more lethal illness; a nuclear event (whether accidental or hostile); and a catastrophic cyber-attack or collapse. Then, of course, there are the properly unknown unknowns which, by definition, cannot be predicted. To look on the bright side, if it is really bad no one will care about the stock market anyway. One person's hoarding is another person's sensible preparedness…

Assuming we are spared Armageddon, there are investment decisions to be made. The first question any financial advisor will ask is about risk tolerance. The chance of higher reward usually comes with higher risk. Invest in a technology start-up and the shares might grow exponentially; they might also drop to be worthless. Invest in a well-established business and the risk is lower, but so is the upside. In general, the younger you are and the more money you have, the more risk you can afford to take. If you are in your twenties in a well-paid job, there is always the chance to make back some of the money you lose, although it would still not be wise to invest all your savings in high-risk investments. Young people investing for retirement have the luxury of a long-time horizon as well as the chance to earn money to make up losses. Someone who is already retired is likely to take a more conservative approach.

Of course, there are never any guarantees, and in the event of one of the catastrophes described above, these rules do not necessarily hold true. The fate suffered by oil company shareholders in 2020 illustrates this point. For example, for decades before 2020, Royal Dutch Shell (RDS) would have been a standard conservative recommendation for an income portfolio. Demand for petroleum was consistent and the company paid a rich dividend varying from 8 to 12%. It was as close to a sure thing as you could get. Then the pandemic came along, conveniently in the middle of the demonisation of fossil fuels, and demand for petroleum dropped more dramatically. Subsequently, RDS shares fell from £22.65 to £10.22. If you are relying on dividend income and have no intention of selling the shares, then share price is just a number. But then, they cut the dividend. For many conservative investors, this was a financial disaster. To make matters worse, the same fate was suffered by several other reliable, traditional dividend-paying companies. In the new normal, even after the end of lockdown, it became apparent that many more people planned to continue to work from home. This reduced demand for formal clothes, cosmetics, workplace canteens, and disturbingly, soap. None of this was predictable as in previous pandemics (like the Spanish flu in 1918), technology was not sufficiently developed for "work from home" to be a plausible solution to the risk of infection. In the meantime, new technology companies like Zoom, previously thought to be risky investments, soared in value during the pandemic and then fell dramatically by late 2021/early 2022.

Diversification: The only way to escape risk completely is to avoid investing in shares and to stick to highly rated bonds and insured bank account deposits. If the zombie apocalypse is really on its way, then land and gold are probably the safest bets (along with bottled water, weapons, and tinned food). Gold is undoubtedly the place that investors go to run and hide when it looks like the world is collapsing. The problem with gold is that gold prices can be highly volatile and gold bars do not pay any return while they are sitting in a vault or under the mattress.

For investors who are prepared to live with some risk, in reward for returns, another way to manage it is diversification. You can diversify according to type of investment, sector, or geography. We have already discussed holding investments other than shares: cash, bonds, gold, and land, so there follows a discussion of sectors and geography.

Sectors and Rotations: The shares of companies in a variety of different industries trade on the stock exchange and they can be grouped into different types or "sectors". There are companies that supply food, household goods, weapons, tobacco, real estate, alcohol, hospitality, luxury goods, technology, pharmaceutical products, commodities, and domestic appliances, just to name a few. The shares in each of these sectors have different characteristics and will go up or down in different ways depending on the state of the economy. During the Covid-19 pandemic, for example, technology shares went up greatly in value, as people relied more heavily on all forms of technology. Shares in food companies remained relatively stable as people always need food. Shares in pharmaceuticals seesawed violently depending on whether the particular company was thought to have found a cure or effective vaccination. And, as discussed above, hospitality and oil shares dropped dramatically. This was a great shock to many investors because oil had always been considered to be in the same category as food; a necessity subject to variation in oil prices but not general falls in the market.

As the vaccination programme rolled out and economies began to reopen, anyone reading the financial press would have heard discussion of a "rotation": different economic circumstances which are likely to lead to different sectors doing particularly well in a given environment. So, for example, in previous pandemics and epidemics, people just took their chances and went to work. No one "worked from home" during the Spanish flu epidemic in 1918 because the technology did not exist. They just went to work and took their chances. In contrast, in the late spring of 2020, it rapidly became apparent that anyone with a desk job (and some other types of jobs as well) was going to rely on technology to work from home and generally keep going. This meant that technology stocks soared: telemedicine, streaming, home delivery and, of course, Zoom, did incredibly well and sometimes even doubled in value. In contrast, the shares in hospitality and aviation companies did very badly and fell substantially in value, as no one knew how long it would take to get back to "normal". Once it became clear that there would be widespread distribution of effective vaccines, these shares began to recover as investors anticipated a re-opening of business and society. Some of the technology shares then fell in value on the assumption that those businesses would do less well when they were needed less, or not at all. This is called a "rotation".

Growth or Dividends? Traditionally, most companies that were doing well paid dividends to shareholders out of their profits. The directors of a company review the financial statements, consider their strategy, and decide whether to declare a dividend or re-invest the profits to carry out research or expand the company's operations. It was rare for a profitable company with a history of paying dividends not to continue to do so. Companies with reliable dividends that increase each year are referred to as "dividend aristocrats" and are favoured by those seeking retirement income. The other advantage of the more traditional dividend paying companies is that they tend to keep paying dividends even when the market is down (2020 being something of an exception). The companies that do not pay dividends tend to be in the technology sector. The focus for these businesses is on increasing the share price or "growth" instead. This is a slightly riskier strategy for the investor because the share price of an individual company that is doing very well can still fall catastrophically if the whole market collapses because of an extraneous event. Moreover, some of newer technology companies may also just turn out to be a bad idea and fail to prosper.

The upside of investing in growth companies is that the returns are far greater when they do well. The highest dividend payers only offer a return of 8-10% (and that is very unusual) whereas a well-timed purchase in the right growth shares can deliver a much higher return, sometimes even doubling in a year (also unusual). No one pays a 100% dividend. The advantage for the younger investor is the very absence of income, as the income would be taxed and might result in entering a higher tax bracket. The "paper" gains (also called unrealised gains) when shares go up in value are not taxed until the shares are sold and the profit is received by the investor. Younger investors can also afford to take more risk, especially if they still have earning capacity, although they will also need a capacity to cope with market volatility. The market routinely drops 10% and growth shares may fall even more dramatically. For example, look at the rise and fall of technology shares from the period of March 2020 through March 2022 (Netflix and Pinterest being two examples). Losses can be very bad for one's blood pressure, even if they are only on paper. For this reason, it is not a good idea to put money that is needed in the short term into the stock market.

Geography: Many investors choose to stay within their home jurisdiction and only trade shares which are denominated in their home currency. This avoids exchange rate risks but can be very limiting if there are opportunities elsewhere. One solution is to invest in a fund that trades in the home currency but invests in other countries. The value of the fund will still reflect currency fluctuations, but not as directly, especially if the managers have taken measures to hedge against the risk.

Defensive Investing: Defensive investing has traditionally meant buying shares in companies that sell things or provide services that are essential and will be needed no matter what the market. These companies tend to be low growth but do provide a reliable dividend that will ensure the investment keeps pace with inflation. Unfortunately, this philosophy has proved very difficult during recent market volatility. Banks crashed in 2008, blue chip oil companies crashed in 2020, and so forth. There are funds that target capital preservation, rather than growth, but even they did not do well in 2020/2021, although the sector reacted better to the Ukraine crisis. A sure thing is very hard to find…

Shares or Funds? Investors have the choice to invest directly in shares or to buy shares in a professionally managed fund, which will try to "best the market" but not always succeed. There are all sorts of funds which specialise in different areas: commodities (such as copper or lithium); funds that specialise according to geography (emerging market or Asia) and that specialise in sectors (pharmaceutical, technology, etc.). Furthermore, there are more general funds and those that are specialised. "Tracker" or "Index" funds are relatively inexpensive and simply track a particular stock market, such as the New York or London Stock Exchanges. An investment company called

Vanguard is probably the best known provider of these funds. As the stock market has historically gone up in excess of inflation, this works as a concept. Exchange Traded Funds (ETFs) will track a particular commodity or group of companies. For example, one of the ETF companies that did extremely well in the aftermath of the pandemic is ARK, which concentrates on new and disruptive technologies. The advantage of a good fund is that the professional managers will be more knowledgeable in the shares that they pick, which can be especially useful if you know nothing about the process. The downside is that funds charge fees for their services, whether the fund does well or not. Some funds are also less liquid than shares and are traded on a weekly rather daily basis, making it difficult to get out quickly if the market is falling and you are inclined to sell. Funds are useful for investors who are not interested in picking shares, don't have time to follow the market or are prevented by their employers from investing directly in shares (some bankers and lawyers). Finally, funds may also have the option to invest in private companies which have not yet come to the stock market, something which is difficult for the small, private investor.

Funds often come with two choices: income or accumulation. The income option will, as the name suggests, pay out income. With the accumulation version, any rise in the value of the shares stays in the "wrapper" of the fund, avoiding income tax liability until the shares in the fund are sold at a later date. To the extent that large dividends are retained in an accumulation fund, some income tax may technically be payable (based on what is called a "notional distribution") to the extent that it exceeds the fund holder's tax-free allowance. If the fund is held with an investment platform or stockbroker, the declaration of income would be contained in the end of year tax statements supplied by them. For this reason, accumulation funds tend to focus more on "growth" shares, although it is not unknown to have a mixture of different equities. For the same reason, Income funds rarely offer an accumulation option. Speaking very generally, accumulation funds tend to be the better option for someone with another source of income (such as employment) who wants to save for the future but does not want to pay higher income taxes in the present.

Chapter Four: Sources of Information and How to Invest

It is difficult for anyone born after 1985 to imagine what life was like before the internet. To find out anything, you had to either go to the library or buy a book or newspaper. There was no Bloomberg, no Google and there was certainly no trading on retail investment platforms using smartphones. The only other option was to pay someone, in this case, a professional money manager, for their advice. Information for the general public was sent by companies to the stock exchange and then released "over the wire" through a device known as a tickertape machine. This machine would sit in stockbrokers' offices, bank and old-fashioned men's clubs slowly spitting out a long ream of paper which showed company news and share prices. Tickertape can still be seen in old films where it was recycled as a form of confetti thrown from tall buildings onto parades in New York. The news would then appear the following day, rather late if it was anything important, in the Financial Times and the Wall Street Journal. After the introduction of the large, live business news screen, there was brief period when there was an incredible dissonance between the market professionals and the retail investor. The private individual still had to rely on tickertape and newspapers while the professional had access to minute-by-minute updates.

We have now come almost full circle. Professionals still have access to high-speed trading platforms and use algorithms that can even trade for them, but there is an enormous amount of real-time and other information available to the private investor. Any internet search will turn up a wealth of information about a given company as well as an up-to-the minute share price. The internet provides, for free, background information on a company, annual reports, and links to analyst reports, share price targets and more. If anything, there is a danger of being overwhelmed or falling prey to dodgy services which claim to offer miraculous profits. Moreover, the average smartphone has a built-in app to follow share prices on a watch list. Many of the more reputable services also offer free watch lists to keep track of selected companies. Still, random scrolling through the internet is probably not a good way to choose investments, although it may be an excellent way to carry out follow-up research. The business and money sections of newspapers are now more likely to concentrate on back stories and in-depth news and so still have a role to play. The money sections will even make recommendations and offer examples of portfolios.

Wealth Managers: For those with large sums to invest or little time to manage their own affairs, there are a plethora of private banks and money managers who will take on the task, for a fee, of course. As with the fund managers, the fee is payable whether or not the portfolio does well and it may be as much as 5%, which is considerable and not even tax deductible in the U.K. A key question is whether the manager or bank has a record of beating the market. If not, the investor might be better off with a low-cost tracker fund. Another problem is that the superstar private wealth managers tend to work only for those with very large sums to invest. Another option is the independent financial advisor, ideally one paid by the hour rather than someone trying to sell a particular product. A good advisor should discuss budget, goals, tax status, risk tolerance and the expectation of income from other sources (such as an inheritance) before advising on a portfolio structure. Finally, time with an accountant to discuss tax implications is always well spent and is also tax deductible.

Ready-made portfolios and robo-investing: There are various alternatives to paying a financial advisor. Some investment platforms, such as Hargreaves Lansdown, have "ready-made" portfolios which recommend shares, and shares in funds, based on a questionnaire about goals and circumstances. The investor is free to follow the recommendations and buy the shares or adjust the portfolio and then retain control of the shares. There is no charge, but the platform hopes the investor will go in to buy the shares using their services. Stockbroker and investment platforms both charge a small commission for using their services to buy and sell shares.

A very recent development is something called "robo-investing", which has been pioneered by several retail banks. The idea is that the investor fills out a questionnaire and then pays into the fund on a regular savings plan; the money is invested by the bank using an algorithm or "robot". The algorithm decides what shares or funds to buy or sell according to the investor's chosen profile, relieving the investor of the need to follow the market closely or indeed, make any decisions.

Advisory Services: The ability to communicate through the internet has also given rise to several online advisory services, which work in different ways, although they all send out regular communications. They are a good source of free information and can be also used to cross-check each other. A certain amount of information is usually free and thereafter the reader pays a subscription. In some cases, there is a free trial and in others payment is upfront. Some of the services offer information and tools to help you make your own decisions and others actively recommend particular shares. All of them will recommend specific shares to watch and most of them concentrate on shares in individual companies rather than funds. So, for example, *Motley Fool* (both U.S. and U.K.) recommends when to buy and sell shares and provides a back story about the company and explains its financial data. *Investors' Chronicle* has daily articles line and a weekly magazine about both shares and funds, focussed a bit more on long-term investing. *Seeking Alpha* (U.S. shares) is more technical and provides sophisticated data for investors who can make use of it. *Investor's Business Daily* (U.S.) and *Zacks* (U.S.) are somewhat more geared towards active traders in the market. *Morningstar* specialises in rating funds and gives a summary of the top holdings, quite a bit of it for free. A warning: many of these companies have incredibly irritating, relentless, and bizarrely unprofessional advertising. If you sign up, at least you will never feel unloved again. The advantage of these services is that they will go through and find the relevant numbers for you and do the math as well.

Business Section of the Newspaper and Magazines: The business section of the better quality (what used to be called broadsheet) newspapers will cover back stories about companies as well as breaking news. Obviously, it is no longer necessary to buy an actual physical newspaper when everything is available digitally. Newspapers can also cover geo-political events that affect the stock market in greater depth than "business only" news sources. *The Economist*, published weekly, is one of the better sources for this kind of information. This sort of background knowledge can be vital for investors who manage their own portfolios. The most obvious recent example was the evolving story about Covid-19 in the early months of 2020. In January 2020 shares reached all-time highs at the same time news was emerging about a new disease in China. Following share prices alone would not have allowed anyone to make a risk assessment about how likely it was that the virus would reach the rest of the world and the economy. There are also specialist business magazines, like the American publications, *Forbes* and *Fortune*, which are aimed slightly more at people in business, rather than investors.

News Services: In addition to the advisory services, there are a variety of subscription investment newsletters available, mostly weekly. Again, some information is available for free, but users need to subscribe in order to read a whole article. Some of these cover funds, others the market in general. *Citywire* and *Investors' Chronicle* provide general information about the UK market; others such as *Dividend Max* specialise in specific sectors. Most of these are available digitally and some still publish paper copies. There are also a plethora of private individuals trying to make money by publishing their own views on stock picking. Some of these are well-considered, whereas others are simply trying to drive up the price of shares they already hold, so *caveat emptor*!

Other Internet Resources and Apps: These are good sources for breaking news and checking on how the market is doing in the middle of a given day. *Bloomberg* and *CNN* both have apps that provide business news. *Bloomberg* is better known in the business world, but *CNN* provides more free information, although there is still a "pro" upgrade for more complete coverage. Both companies have dedicated television stations and *Bloomberg* even has a radio station. Moreover, just typing in the question "is [name of share] a buy?" will turn up dozens of answers and opinions from analysts, for free.

Many companies also offer webinars about what they are buying and provide views on the market. Cathie Wood of ARK has a monthly Zoom session that anyone can join, and Baillie Gifford (a well-known fund manager) runs frequent webinars that are open to anyone who signs up. Finally, there are a myriad of podcasts by magazines such as *The Economist* as well as those from services such as *Motley Fool*.

With all these resources, it is ultimately for the investor to decide whether the company has a good story, along with the right numbers, and whether the investment seems like a good idea considering social, economic, and political factors taken as a whole. Some basic questions include:

- What is the general view of the share price? Too high? A bargain? Is there a currency risk?
- What is the trend over five years for the share price? In some cases, it has been going down steadily for years. Usually, such companies pay a relatively high dividend,

but at the cost of capital erosion (for an example, look at a share price chart for AT&T from 2016-21). This may not matter if the investor is 95 years old and looking for income, but not a good choice for a young person saving for retirement.
- Has there been a recent development that has affected the company in a good or bad way?
- If the share price has recently gone up dramatically, are you too late to the party? Sudden and dramatic increases are frequently followed by disconcerting falls.
- Is this a dividend or growth-orientated investment?
- How risky is it perceived to be?
- What is the market view on whether to buy, sell or hold?
- Does the company's business sound like a good idea? Or at least, do lots of other people think it is a good idea? Confession: I thought Facebook was a truly terrible idea because who would want to be tortured, at home, by other people continually showing off and pretending to have perfect lives? Everyone, apparently.

Official Documents and Filings: All public companies are required to file audited financial reports and provide other information to both the stock market and shareholders. Most of this is fairly impenetrable and, in any event, a bit late, as it looks back at the previous year or quarter. One of the more interesting filings is the register of directors' interests. Directors are required to let the London Stock Exchange know when they have bought or sold shares in their own company and this information is made available to the public. Directors buying a lot of shares indicates faith in the company. Selling shares could be a bad sign, but in an individual case it could also just mean a need for money for a significant expense.

Tips and Insider Dealing. Do not do this! It is illegal and carries possible criminal convictions. In the old days, insider dealing was rife in the City of London and, in fact, was an important source of income for bankers and stockbrokers. No one had much money because of high taxation and a tip on a share here or there was seen as a perk of working in finance. That was back in the 1970s when it was not illegal. It is illegal now and I cannot put it any more clearly than that. How can you tell if it is illegal insider dealing? It needs to be price sensitive inside information, not known to the public, about shares in a particular company. It can be good news or bad news. So, the fact that a company orders pizza for lunch in the boardroom every day is not price sensitive, even if they used to order sushi. If the company has struck oil, had a ship sink or discovered a cure for cancer, that information is obviously price sensitive. Someone saying the market is a bubble and that share prices are about to collapse is not information about a particular company.

Stockbrokers and other licensed platforms are required to cooperate with government authorities to "look through" to help discover the real owner of shares. This is routine practice whenever the graphs show increased trading ahead of an important announcement.

Reading a share price chart; Bulls and Bears: At a basic level, a simple app included with most smartphones will tell you the current share price and provide other relevant data. It will also give you the opening price for the day, the highest price paid for the day, and the lowest price paid for the day. It will also show the 52 week highest and lowest prices paid. The chart can be changed by tapping on the day, week, month, year, or several years to show the price progression in a graph. Other information includes:

- The *volume* and *average volume*. This is the number of shares traded in a given period of time. Services that issue recommendations based on mathematical formulae place great emphasis on volume as a predictor of when to buy or sell shares.
- The *P/E*. This is the *price to earnings ratio*, calculated as a number. It tends to be sky high in technology companies (sometimes over 100) and much lower in traditional businesses (it can be single digits). There is much discussion about whether companies with higher numbers are overvalued and vice versa.
- The *market capitalisation*. This is simply the number of shares outstanding multiplied by the share price. It gives the total market worth of the company (which may not be what it is actually worth based on assets, cash flow and other considerations).
- The *yield*. This is the dividend of the company expressed as a percentage of the share price. Important for investors looking for income. *Total return* includes both the yield and any increase in the share price.
- The *EPS* (earnings per share). The earnings per share of the company after expenses (net profit).

- The *Beta*. This a volatility calculation. The stock market index has a Beta number of "1". A higher Beta number means the company's share price does not fluctuate in step with the overall market and is more volatile. A lower Beta number means the company share price is less volatile than the market overall. The "*Vix*" is a volatility index that refers to the market as a whole, or sectors of the market. Long-term holders do not like volatility.

Other useful terms: As with any area of life, investing is full of shorthand phrases and jargon. These include the following:

- *"Basis Points"* are used in discussing interest rates. A basis point is equal to 1/100 of a percent.
- "*Bulls*" are people or institutions who are positive about the market; a "*bull market*" is a rising market in which it is easier to make money. "*Bears*" are pessimists who think the market will fall; it is also possible to be "*bearish*" about a particular company or industry.
- Analysts will publish reports that recommend a "*buy*", "*sell*" or "*hold*" about a particular

company. Buy and sell are obvious, the *hold* recommendation means the price is too high to recommend buying anymore but the company is doing well enough that the shares should not be sold. Some investment funds will speak of *"overweight", "market weight"* and *"underweight"*, which mean the same thing.

- *"Buying the Dip"* is waiting for shares in a good company to fall for no good reason (such as a general market correction), and then buying them at a lower price. Of course, it is always difficult to time this, as the shares may keep falling.

- *"Day Trading"* is buying and selling shares actively, over very short periods of time, rather than holding for investment. This is what professional traders do, although there are also individuals (often retired or out of work bankers) who do this from home. It is extremely risky and needs a constant stream of information as well as high speed internet.

- *"Disruptive Technology"* refers to new and innovative technology that threatens to displace or "disrupt" traditional industries. In the early 1900s, the automotive industry would have disrupted carriage manufacturers. Today, the term frequently refers to technology and financial technology companies. For an excellent discussion of the term, see Cathie Wood's presentation in 2019 at the Singularity University Summit on Investing in Disruptive Innovation.

- *"Dividend Cover"* is the ratio of a company's net income over the dividend paid to shareholders. If a company pays a good dividend but has low dividend cover, then the continued payment of a high dividend may be at risk. A dividend cover above "2" is considered good.
- *"Dividend Aristocrat"* is a term used to describe companies that have consistently paid out and increased dividends over the past 25 years. Note: the dividends may not be very high, but they are consistent.
- *"ESG"* stands for environmental, social and governance. Back in the 1980s in the era of the film *Wall Street*, lunch was for wimps, and no one cared about the environment or workers. The world has changed dramatically, led, surprisingly, by large institutional investors. The largest asset management firms and pension funds now insist that companies show evidence of their commitment to ESG as a condition of investing in them. The chairman of the asset

management firm BlackRock even publishes an open letter on the subject annually. This means that the share price of companies that do not embrace ESG will fall because large and powerful investors will refuse to buy their shares, creating less demand. ESG is obviously difficult to measure but the pressure is being felt across nearly all industries, particularly those that are carbon intensive (such as oil companies) or those considered to be morally dubious in some way (such as tobacco companies).

- *"Fractional shares"* are exactly what they sound like: fractions of shares. These can also be traded and are useful for those with relatively small sums to invest, who would like to invest in companies with expensive shares.
- To be "*long*" a company needs to own a significant percentage compared to the other holdings in the portfolio, leaving the investor possibly over-exposed to the risks of that one business.
- The most ridiculous term of all is "*market correction*", which is a euphemism for a drop in the market, as if it had been wrong previously when everyone was cheerful that their shares were doing well. This is used by

professional money managers to say that "the market has corrected", rather than "you just lost a lot of money".

- *"Meme stocks"* are shares that get caught up in a short selling roller coaster where small private investors bid up the price of shares that have been sold short, knowing that when the short sellers go into the market to buy shares to cover their short sales, they will then have to pay a premium.
- An *"option"* is an option to buy or sell shares at a given price at some point in the future.
- *"Short selling"* is a way to make money if an investor thinks that the company's shares are likely to fall in the future. In brief, the seller agrees with a counterparty that they will sell the party shares in a company, at today's price, at a date in the future. At this point, the seller does own the shares that they are going to sell. So, if the shares are worth £8 a share today and they fall to £5 a share next week, the seller buys them next week at £5 a share in the market and then sells them as agreed at £8 a share, making a profit of £3 a share. (Obviously, the counterparty must hold the opposite view of the company's prospects.). Companies absolutely hate it when their shares are sold

short as it sends a bad message to the market. Recently, Tesla was targeted with a bout of short selling. The price did not fall, and the short sellers lost a lot of money. Elon Musk then sent them all shorts; bright red shorts, with "the short shorts" printed on them.

- A *"Stop Loss Order"* is an order left with a broker to sell automatically if the shares fall to a given price to limit losses.
- In contrast a *"Stop Limit Order"* is an order to buy, once shares reach a given price.
- *Tax Wrapper* refers to tax protected investments such as a pension, SIPP, or ISA. No tax is payable on income or capital gains on investments while they are in the tax wrapper.
- The best resource for more information on financial vocabulary is a website called *Investopedia.* There are also some wonderful explanations on a YouTube channel featuring a man called Paddy Hirsh, who takes it upon himself to explain all manner of financial terms in short, entertaining clips.

How to Invest: The Mechanics

Traditional Brokers: Traditional stockbrokers buy and sell shares on behalf of their clients, taking a commission for each transaction. In America, stockbrokers will also play an advisory role, discussing the merits of additional investments with clients without charging a management fee. In the UK, this service would only be offered with a fee for discretionary management. Stockbrokers are usually contacted by email or telephone. Some stockbrokers are independent, while others are connected to retail banks or money managers.

Online Brokers: Online brokers are a recent and very popular development who also charge commission for transactions. Online brokers make it easy for people with only a small amount to invest. The difference is that the clients place the trades themselves, over the internet, using the online broker as a platform. Fees and service levels vary. This allows retail investors to manage their portfolios directly, without an intermediary. Both "stop loss" and "stop limit" orders can be placed through online brokers, without the need for any human interaction. The downside of online brokers is that the platforms sometimes develop technological problems, making it difficult to trade. The upside, besides the lower fees, is that orders can be placed 24/7, although they will only be fulfilled when the relevant market opens.

Timing and Cost-Averaging: Timing the market and deciding when to buy shares in a particular company can be challenging. It is very disheartening to invest and then watch the shares plummet in value, whether because of poor earnings or extraneous forces. Most commentators stress the importance of holding for long-term investment; time *in* the market rather than timing the market. One way to even out the risk is cost-averaging or investing slowly over a period of time, such as a year. For most salaried investors this happens naturally, as savings are accumulated each month. However, in the case of a sudden windfall or inheritance, it is worth considering whether it would be wise to spread out investment purchases. The exception would be a situation where it is obvious that share prices in a particular sector are likely to skyrocket because of geopolitical or other factors. For example, in spring 2020, it didn't take a financial genius to realise that shares of companies that made disinfectant bleach (Clorox) and home entertainment (Netflix) were going up, at least temporarily. Thankfully, however, pandemics are not a frequent occurrence.

Profit Taking: If shares in a company have really "popped" and doubled or tripled in value over a very short time, there is always the question of whether it is wise to "take a little off the table" and take profits, lest the shares decline equally precipitously. Stock markets can be irrational and pile into shares out of fear of missing out and because it seems like a good idea at the time. When the market realises that the people running the company are only human after all, the price falls back down to earth. It can be tricky to predict the top, but in these situations, it may be wise to sell some of the shares and take the profit, while keeping the original sum invested. So, you buy 50 shares in August, at $200 per share ($10,000). In October, the share price rises to $390 a share ($19,500). You sell 12 shares ($4,680), keeping the rest invested. The share price then falls to $233 in November 2021, when it turns out that owning the shares does not grant you eternal life, but you have taken the profits while keeping some of your shares, which are still worth more than the original investment.

Bed and Breakfast: Once upon a time, a very popular practice was to sell shares when they rose, and then buy them back when they dipped. Or, to sell them on the last day of the tax year in order to take advantage of your tax-free capital gains allowance, and then buy them back the next day. Sadly, this is no longer the useful practice that it once was. In the U.K., if you buy and sell and buy the same shares within a twelve-month period, any gains will be taxed as ordinary income and will not benefit from capital gain treatment. However, this rule does not apply if the shares are then repurchased within the "tax wrapper" of an ISA or SIPP. So, one option is to "bed an ISA", in other words, sell on the last day of a tax year and buy them back in your ISA, using your new annual ISA allowance.

Chapter Five: ISAs, SIPPs and Taxes

"...in this world, nothing is certain except death and taxes" (Benjamin Franklin, 1789)

There is no option but to pay your taxes or be fined, or worse: spend time in prison. What is clear, however, is that understanding your tax affairs can make an enormous financial difference. What is not so clear is that there are all sorts of taxes at all sorts of different rates that apply in different situations. Accordingly, the following discussion comes with an extremely important disclaimer; these general remarks should only be taken as a very vague example of the importance of managing your tax liability, rather than as any kind of advice. Nothing should be relied on without independent verification. Rates change so frequently that the numbers quoted below could almost be hypothetical. The point of this section is to show that different types of income are taxed at different rates (or not at all), and in different ways. As an example, for a self-employed person, deciding whether to take income in the form of salary paid or dividends can make a significant difference as to tax liability. The good news is that a well-qualified accountant can help to optimise the situation; moreover, tax-related accountancy fees are tax-deductible.

ISAs

At the time of writing, the tax authorities in the U.K. permit two main ways to invest without paying taxes, at least in the short term. These investment schemes are designed by the government to encourage citizens to save, variously, for rainy days, house deposits and retirement.

An ISA is an individual savings account in which up to £20,000 a year can be invested, with no tax on income or gains. An ISA can be cash or shares. A SIPP is a self-invested personal pension, with a lifetime limit of £1 million cash invested. A brokerage account is simply an account through which shares are traded, with no tax advantages. Both ISAs and SIPPs have tax advantages, although they differ in significant ways.

ISA and Lifetime ISA: Anyone can contribute up to £20,000 a year to an ISA. The money can come from any source: gifts, salary, dividends, or capital gains. The unique selling point of the ISA is that any gains are tax-free, with no limit, whether they are income or capital gains. So, it makes sense for anyone with a lump sum to put an additional £20,000 into the ISA every year. In fact, it would be financial insanity for anyone with spare cash not to have an ISA as the money can be withdrawn at any time. ISAs can be cash or shares. If they are set up through a retail trading platform, the shares can easily be managed online by the investor. Once taken out of the ISA, the money withdrawn cannot be put back, unless it is part of the £20,000 in a new tax year.

A Lifetime ISA ("LISA") is slightly different. A LISA is designed to help younger people buy their first homes, up to the value of £450,000. Only £4,000 a year can be contributed, but that amount is "grossed up" by 25% by the government, so an investment of £4,000 would wind up being £5,000. However, there are several restrictions. A LISA can only be opened by people between the ages of 18 and 39, although it is possible to keep paying in until the age of 60. Investments can be shares or cash. The money cannot be taken out, except for a home purchase, before the age of 60. The money is tax-free if used for the purchase of a home or taken out after the age of 60, otherwise, there are penalties. The money cannot be used as a deposit on a house worth more than £450,000, so it is not an easy way for very wealthy families to add to the value of a deposit for a more expensive home. The £450,000 limit does go up if there are joint buyers, although two LISAs can be combined to buy a less expensive property. You are, however, allowed to have a LISA alongside a regular ISA. So, if you are flush with cash and between the ages of 18 and 39 and have already used up the £20,000 allowance for the regular ISA, it might make sense to add on a LISA as a kind of additional retirement savings. Put simply, the money in a LISA is grossed up by 25% by the government in the same way as it is in a SIPP, however, unlike a SIPP, the money in the LISA can be taken out tax free after the age of 60.

SIPPs

SIPP: A SIPP is a self-invested personal pension plan, designed primarily for those with an income from employment or self-employment. Unlike a workplace pension, you cannot "salary sacrifice" to reduce your taxable income, however, the government does gross up the amount paid in by the investor's marginal tax rate. Once having opened a SIPP, an individual has the right to contribute the greater of £3,600 or 100% of their salary up to a limit of £40,000 a year. This can be in a lump sum or by regular contributions. Even someone with no employment income is entitled to contribute up to £3,600 a year. The government will then gross up that amount at the individual's marginal tax rate. So, if an investor with a marginal tax rate of 20% puts £5,000 in a SIPP, the SIPP balance will then show £6,000, with the £1,000 having been contributed by the government to make up for the tax that was paid on that money. The idea is to put the individual in approximately the same position as an employee with a workplace pension where contributions are deducted before tax. Of course, it isn't quite as good, both because there are no employer contributions and because the gross salary amount before SIPP contributions is higher, so more NI is paid, higher student loan repayments may be due, and so forth. Once the money is in the SIPP, it can be invested in shares, bonds, funds, or a variety of other investments (excluding residential property), or simply left in cash. No tax is payable on any income or capital gains if it all stays in the SIPP. One of the advantages of a SIPP is that the holder can take out up to 25%, free of tax, after the age of 55.

Disadvantages:
1. SIPPs turned out to be very successful once they were introduced and the government began to gradually claw back some of the

benefits and the amount that could be invested. There is a lifetime allowance for the value of the pension pot of £1,073,100. So, if someone in a very successful job contributed £40,000 a year for 30 years, the SIPP would be worth £1,200,000, which would put it over the limit, even without investing.

2. There are serious tax penalties for early withdrawal from a SIPP and so it is really only useful for retirement planning. As noted above, after the age of 55 (57 after 2028), up to 25% can be withdrawn tax-free. Any further withdrawals are taxed at the individual's income tax rate at the time.

Ready-made SIPPs are offered by a large number of different financial service providers. SIPPs can be set up with most online trading platforms, in these cases the investors manage the portfolio directly. Alternately, a variety of companies offer readymade SIPPs, although of course they charge a fee. The performance of these companies varies considerably, and the investor would be wise to check the fund's performance relative to competitors and the market as a whole.

Which is better? Large contributions to a SIPP can only be made from earned income; people who are not currently employed (who might well have income from other sources) are limited to £3,600 a year. For those who are not in the workforce, an ISA may be the only option. Withdrawals from a SIPP can only be made after the age of 55 (whereas they can be made from an ISA at any time). At this point, the investor can withdraw up to 25% of the value of the SIPP free of tax. The problem is that thereafter, SIPP withdrawals (whether income or capital gains) are taxed as ordinary income at the taxpayer's normal rate of income tax, whereas ISA withdrawals are entirely tax free, at any time.

Which is more efficient? For higher earners, the SIPP may allow greater contributions (remember ISAs are limited to £20,000 a year) and a gross up from the government. It depends on how much money there is available to invest. For someone with £20,000 a year to invest, who expects a large inheritance or has a company pension which will give them a retirement income of over £50,000 a year, the ISA might be better because SIPP withdrawals will be taxed and may push the person into a higher tax bracket. It would also then be possible to remain a basic rate taxpayer and so pay capital gains tax at a lower rate while enjoying tax-free withdrawals from an ISA. For someone with an inheritance or other funds who has stopped working because of family commitments, the ISA is the option which will allow the greatest amount of tax-free investing. For those in work, there is more to invest in the first place with a SIPP because of the extra 25% added to the pot by the government, and there is also the 25% withdrawal that can be taken free of tax. For these people, a calculation will need to be made about whether the extra money invested will offset a higher rate of income and capital gains tax. Finally, the amount in a SIPP can be left tax free to heirs if the taxpayer dies before the age of 75. Ultimately, it depends on individual circumstances and accounting advice should be taken.

Brokerage Account: For the fortunate individual who still has money left over after investing in an ISA and perhaps, a SIPP, there are ordinary brokerage accounts where shares can be bought and sold. Taxes are paid on the income and capital gains in the normal way. Losses (when a share is sold for less than the purchase price) can be carried forward indefinitely and set off against current or future capital gains. The "wash-sale" rules mean that it is not possible to sell a share, take the loss and then buy it back within 30 days.

Taxes

The government retains the right to change tax rates and increase them at any given time;

needless to say, this can make it rather difficult to budget. In the biblical story in Genesis, the Egyptian Pharaoh's dreams were interpreted by Joseph to mean that there would be seven good years followed by seven lean years. Pharaoh was advised to put aside grain and other food during the good times as a reserve for later periods of hardship. He followed Joseph's advice and Egypt survived the famine that laid waste to other nations. Bizarrely, the wisdom of this ancient story seems to have escaped present day politicians. The modern practice is to spend whatever is available during the good times and raise taxes (or eliminate universal benefits) whenever there is difficulty. In effect, the government uses the wealth and earnings of those who are even slightly better off as a savings account for a rainy day. It is, however, possible to do things differently; the Norwegian government used its North Sea oil wealth to establish a sovereign wealth fund, which is now one of the most powerful investors in the world (although they seem to have high taxes anyway).

Income Tax: Income tax is paid on earned income (salaries). It is also payable on interest from bank accounts and some bonds. For the self-employed, business related expenses are tax deductible. For employees, tax is withheld from salaries at source in the form of the Pay As You

Earn scheme (PAYE). This means that self-employed people have an obligation to file a tax return and will normally face a tax bill twice a year. Salaried employees with no other source of income will not ordinarily face other tax charges. Needless to say, without condoning the practice, "business expenses" have been known to be construed widely by self-employed taxpayers. NI, which is not insignificant, is also deducted from pay at source. At the time of writing:

- Everyone has a tax-free personal allowance of £12,570 until they begin to make over £100,000 a year.
- The basic rate of taxation, 20%, applies to earnings from £12,571 to £50,270. This is supposed to drop to 19% in 2023.
- Higher rate taxation of 40% applies to earnings from £50,271 to £150,000. However, once over £100,000, the taxpayer starts to lose the £12,570 personal allowance, which can leave the victim paying a 60% marginal tax rate.
- Income of over £150,000 is taxed at 45%.

What is more, moving into a higher tax bracket can mean the loss of benefits such as child benefit as well as paying a higher rate of tax on capital gains. Strategic salary sacrifice into a pension (as discussed above) can be very useful for employees in postponing the move into a higher tax bracket until there are more meaningful gains. It also has the effect of reducing student loan payments. A pay rise of £2,000 from £50,000 a year to £52,000 a year might not really be worth it, unless saved directly into a pension. It might seem like a solution to take benefits in kind instead of salary, but these too need to be declared, although it might still be less than the amount that an individual would pay otherwise. In the case of private medical insurance, for example, employers benefit from group rates which are likely to be cheaper than what an individual would pay; there are also some other concessions. Benefits in kind are also exempt from NI tax, which is not insignificant.

National Insurance: NI adds to the tax burden at quite a significant level. Unfortunately, because it is called "national insurance" rather than "income tax", governments that were elected on a promise not to raise taxes do not feel this means they cannot raise the rate of NI. NI has recently been increased by 1.25%, which will have a real impact on take-home salaries. NI is paid by both employers and employees, although at different rates. The advantage of NI is that anyone who has worked and paid NI for 35 years is entitled to a state pension at some point in their late 60s (getting later all the time…). Given that the current state pension is currently £179.60 a week, this isn't much consolation.

Dividend Tax and Savings Tax: Dividend and savings income are taxed under a separate regime from earned income. The theoretical justification for this is that money invested in companies has presumably already been taxed at least once, whatever the source. Many people reliant on dividend income are retired and unable to "work harder or longer" to make up for an income lowered by tax rises. Moreover, the government wants to encourage investment and so provides a bit of tax reward for putting money into companies rather than leaving it in a bank. There is a tax-free allowance for the first £2,000 of dividend income. In line with the recently announced increase in NI payments, dividend tax has also been increased, with effect from April 2022. Thereafter, basic rate payers are liable for tax at 8.75%, higher rate payers at 33.75% and additional rate payers at 39.35%. For interest on savings, there is an allowance of £1,000 for basic rate payers, £500 for additional rate payers and none for higher rate payers. 39.35% is a pretty steep tax rate for someone who has paid taxes through their working life and saved, hoping for a prosperous retirement, out of what is left over. It illustrates the importance of saving in an ISA for anyone who might fall into this category.

Capital Gains Tax: Capital gains tax is paid on the profits from the sale of shares or other assets, excluding the taxpayer's principal residence. Capital gains tax is not inflation linked. If someone bought an asset for £100 in 1950 and then sold it for £1 million pounds today, that person would be liable for tax on the full £999,000, assuming that is all profit. All taxpayers currently have a tax-free capital gains allowance of £12,500. After that, the rate of tax is 10% for basic rate taxpayers and 20% for higher and additional rate taxpayers. Capital gains tax differs from other taxes in that losses can be offset against gains. In the U.K., losses can be carried forward indefinitely; in other words, the sale of shares at a big loss can be carried forward to offset gains in future years.

Inheritance and Gift Tax: All estates have a tax-free allowance of £325,000. Thereafter, tax is payable at 40%. This is an enormous sum when you realise that the decedent has already paid income and other taxes on whatever wealth has been acquired during the person's lifetime. The 40% is paid by the estate, not any of the beneficiaries. So, the estate is taxed at 40% whether there are two beneficiaries or dozens.

Putting assets into a trust might seem to be an obvious solution. The trust then becomes the legal owner and there is no change of ownership and therefore no tax on the death of one of the beneficiaries. The tax authorities have put a stop to this loophole by taxing transfers into a trust at 20%; less than inheritance tax but still painful, especially for those who need the full value of their assets in retirement. Putting assets into a trust on your deathbed, just before they switch off the life support, also doesn't count. The transfer into trust needs to be made at least seven years before death to attract the lower rate of 20%. In the absence of ethics, it could come down to a calculation of the cost of life support versus the tax savings. On the brighter side, all gifts given more than seven years before the decedent's death are tax-free, as are all gifts to spouses, civil partners, or charities. Regular maintenance payments to children (even if they are adults) are also exempt from gift tax.

VAT: Value Added Tax (VAT) is a sales tax added at varying rates to all goods and services which are not deemed essential. VAT is payable on restaurant meals, but there is no VAT payable on food, whether it be filet steak or beans, unless it is confectionery. Confectionery is a luxury. Probably the most famous VAT case was about whether a Jaffa cake was a cake (a staple food, so no VAT) or a biscuit (frivolous non-essential food item attracting VAT). It came down to the fact that Jaffa cakes get stale, like a cake, and so, therefore, are a cake. Thus, cake is legally and officially a staple food. This is absolutely the most (single, only?) cheerful thing about VAT.

Stamp Duty: Stamp duty is payable by the buyer upon the purchase of a property. The rate payable can be punitive and depends on the cost of the property and whether it is a primary residence, as opposed to a second home or investment property. The unfortunate side effect of this tax is that it makes it more expensive and difficult to move house, especially in expensive areas like London. It also dissuades older people from downsizing and freeing up larger family houses, as a large chunk of wealth will be taken up in stamp duty paid for the next home.

Council Tax: Council tax is levied by individual councils and varies widely. There is an exemption for students and discounts are available for disabled people and for single-person households. Other exemptions may be available depending on the local authority.

Other Taxes: Other taxes, such as a wealth tax, are always being mooted. Other than literally hiding the money under the mattress or breaking the law and putting it in a bank secrecy jurisdiction, there is no solution to taxation but to exercise your right to vote. At least, read the paragraph above on VAT and go eat some cake while it is still possible to do so.

Chapter Six: Borrowing Money and Home Ownership

All commercial loans work on the same principle: the lender lends money to the borrower and the borrower pays the lender interest to compensate for the loss of the use of the money and for the risk of loss. In theory, the higher the risk of loss, the higher the interest rate should be. The interest rate will also reflect the lender's view of the likely trend of inflation. If inflation is high, the lender will demand a higher rate of interest to compensate for the fact that the money will be worth less when it is returned. Interest rates can be fixed for the term of the loan at the time of borrowing or they can be "floating". Floating or variable rates will vary according to a particular public rate, such as the basic rate set by the central bank or the rate at which banks lend to each other. Usually, floating rate loans are a certain percentage over the rate to which they are linked.

Unsecured Borrowing: Other than student loans, most significant borrowing will require some collateral for the lender. Unsecured borrowing, such as credit cards or payday loans, tends to have much, much higher rates of interest than a bank loan. The interest compounds monthly and can leave the borrower paying back multiples of the original amount borrowed. In the case of a large purchase, it is worth shopping around to look for interest-free credit. The real problem comes when people live beyond their means, seduced by the endless "buy now, pay later" on websites and wind up maxing out their credit cards and only paying off the interest monthly. This is not the road to financial prosperity or even just a good credit rating.

Credit Rating and Why to Have a Credit Card: This is a measure of the borrower's creditworthiness, or how likely they are to repay a loan based on past history. Building up debts and missing payments will all damage a borrower's credit rating, making it more difficult to get other important loans in the future. Not having a credit rating at all can also be a problem. Having at least one credit card, in your sole name (even after marriage), and paying it off in full every month is one way to build a good credit rating.

A credit card will also offer some degree of protection for poor service or inadequate goods purchased on the card. Another advantage is that many cards offer vouchers or other benefits based on the money spent.

Student Loans: the student loan system is both a morass and a moving target, as the government makes frequent changes. The best solution to determine what is best in an individual situation is to check one of the excellent money management websites, which stay up to date with changes and will gently lead even the most math-phobic arts student through the numbers. Money Saving Expert is particularly helpful. (See further information here).

Here are some general observations:

1. Unlike student loans in the U.S., the student borrower only needs to repay the loan when in employment and making over a certain amount of money (however, the threshold amount keeps changing). If you are badly paid, unemployed, stop work because of caring responsibilities, become too ill to work or just want go lie on a beach, the loan is paused and repayments do not need to be made during that period. Student loans are also cancelled upon the death of the borrower.

2. Loan repayments are deducted from, and based on, salaries, not capital gains or inheritance. Savings and dividend income do count for student loan income calculation. Selling an app for millions, winning the lottery, or inheriting a fortune do not. Not a very useful loophole, but still.

3. The amount of interest payable, the interest rate and the terms of the loan vary according to when it was taken out and whether it was used for undergraduate or postgraduate education.

4. The amount of interest charged on the loan varies according to the official rate of inflation, the Retail Prices Index (RPI). The rate of interest varies from RPI to RPI plus 3%, depending on the amount earned and the date on which the loan was taken out. This is so that the amount borrowed is not wiped out by inflation rises in the future.

5. However, the amount payable in any year is never more than 9% of the borrower's income over the initial payment threshold, even if inflation goes up to 15%.

6. The loan is written off after a period of time; until recently this was 25 years after the first repayment became due, although the government has now proposed extending this to 40 years. The effect of this extension will be that

lower paid borrowers will actually wind up paying far more, as the capital amount of the loan will be outstanding for longer. Previously, many loans would have been written off long before repayment. In contrast, the higher paid will pay off their loans more quickly and so wind up paying less.

7. Borrowers can repay the loan in full at any time, although it may not always be financially advisable to do so. In particular, anyone who plans to work in a low paid occupation (the voluntary sector, religion, etc.) or spend long periods at home parenting or caring would be better off not repaying the loan.

8. In practice, only higher earners wind up repaying their loans in full.

9. It is a truth universally acknowledged that the bureaucracy is horrendous and communicating with the Student Loans Company is a nightmare.

Mortgages: Most buyers are unable to put down cash for the full amount of a property and take out a "mortgage" instead. A mortgage means that a bank lends money to the buyer and takes a lien or mortgage on the house as security or collateral for the money lent. The bank will normally insist on a survey to establish the value of a property to make sure that its money is safe. If the loan repayments are not made, the bank then has the right to seize the property and sell it to get its money back. This point will be made repeatedly by the lender and the lawyers involved. There are several other issues which are not always so well explained. These include:

1. **Fixed or Variable Rate Interest**? The repayment terms will be based on either a fixed or floating rate of interest. A fixed rate means that the rate is fixed for the term of the mortgage at, for example, 5% of the amount borrowed. A variable or floating rate is when the rate goes up and down according to an external interest rate, such as the rate fixed by a central bank.

2. **Are there Repayment Penalties**? The bank makes its money by lending it out and charging interest. Banks like to know that they can depend on that steady stream of income. Moreover, if interest rates decline, it is very valuable for the bank to have loans outstanding at a higher rate. If interest rates decline from 6% to 2% and stay there for years, and the bank is able to charge interest on 20-year loans to mortgage payers at 6% and then pay out 2% on savings accounts, the bank will be very happy. Of course, the borrower would want to transfer the mortgage to another provider or arrange

different terms. For this reason, mortgages frequently contain "pre-payment penalties" which mean that it can be more expensive to repay a mortgage early.

3. **Portability:** Is it possible to sell the property and substitute another one on the same terms? Obviously, the new property would have to be subject to a survey, but this is still a question worth asking.

4. **What are the Fees**? A borrower might think that the bank is getting enough money in the form of interest but there are also arrangement fees for the cost of setting up the mortgage. In addition, there are surveyors' fees and lawyers' fees to be aware of.

5. **Negative Equity:** This is what happens when the property falls in value and is worth less than the mortgage. This isn't an immediate problem unless the homeowner needs to sell the property. The borrower not only loses money on the sale but remains liable for the full amount of the mortgage and will have to continue repayments over and above the amount received for the sale.

6. **Insurance:** The bank will insist on buildings insurance (a good idea anyway) and upon being noted in the policy. The insurance is not for the full amount paid for the property because that

includes the value of the land and the location; the insurance is for the rebuilding cost.

7. **Deposit and Affordability:** After a credit check, the bank will normally insist on some form of cash deposit so that they are not lending the full value of the property. The amount the bank is prepared to lend on top of the deposit will be a multiple of the after-tax (and after other loan payments) income of the buyer. In some cases, the bank will make a more adventurous loan if there is a third-party guarantee.

8. **Term and Repayment:** The term of the loan is the number of years it will take to repay the loan, normally between 20 and 30 years. It may also be possible to take a non-repayment interest-only loan, where only interest on the capital is paid and there are no actual repayments.

9. **Title Check and Land Registry:** These are standard but important checks to make sure that the seller actually owns the property and isn't just renting it or running a scam.

10. **Freehold or Leasehold:** Freehold property is owned outright, although of course, this is subject to local authority rules and planning restrictions. It is more common for houses, rather than flats, to be freehold, although flats may also be sold with a share of the freehold.

Leasehold property is not the same as renting. It is a (usually) long lease held from a landlord known as the "freeholder". The lease may be as long as 999 years or as short as five or six years. Long leases of over 100 years sell for a similar price as a freehold property. Once the term of the lease falls below 85 or 90 years, the value begins to decline with time. This can be a problem if the buyer is seeking a long-term mortgage. Some (but not all) leases come with the right to "enfranchise" or buy the freehold, for a negotiated price. Finally, there are two significant disadvantages to leaseholds: first, the leaseholder needs to have the landlord's consent before making alterations to the property; the landlord will usually charge for this. Second, the freeholder will charge "ground rent"; an annual fee that will normally increase over time. Thus, legal advice should be sought on all these points and on the costs involved.

11. **Joint Ownership.** It is now common for couples to own property together without first getting married. If done properly, this is much more complicated than a purchase by a married couple. If a married couple separates, divorce imposes a legal division of property and financial responsibility. The same is true in the case of death; in a marriage with no children, in the

absence of a will there are automatic rights of inheritance. None of this is true for those who are just living together and all need to be worked out with a lawyer. There are different types of joint ownership and legal advice would need to be taken before choosing which one was most suitable. Further information about these rights is provided below:

Tenants in Common
1. No automatic right of inheritance if the other dies
2. Can own different percentages of the property
3. Can leave their interest in the party to a third party in a will
4. Need to make express provisions and agreements about sale of interest

Joint Tenants
1. Have equal property rights
2. Automatically inherit if the other dies
3. Cannot leave the property to someone else in a will
4. Cannot sell an interest in the property without the consent of the other

12. **Help to Buy and Shared Ownership.** The government's **Help to Buy** scheme is designed to help first-time buyers who have had difficulty

putting together more than 5% as a deposit. The current scheme only runs until March 2023 and it remains to be seen whether it will be replaced by something similar. The government will lend prospective home buyers up to 20% of the cost of a newly built home, and up to 40% in London. The borrower can then apply for a normal commercial mortgage for the rest of the purchase price and the usual terms and conditions will apply. Note that the scheme is restricted to those buying a newly built home. This makes it considerably less useful as most of the housing stock in cities is older. There are also price limits on the home that can be bought using the scheme: £600,000 in London, although considerably less in other regions.

Shared Ownership is slightly different. The current scheme offers buyers with an income below a certain threshold (currently £90,000 a year) a chance to buy a fractional interest (as low as 10%) in a home and pay rent on the remaining share. The remaining share can then be acquired incrementally, in amounts as low as 1%. Of course, paying rent may make it impossible to save enough money to buy the remaining share, but the idea is that the buyer will at least then have some interest in the property market and be able to profit from rising prices. It might be possible, for example, to own a fractional interest in a home in London which could then be sold later and used to buy an entire dwelling somewhere further out, where prices are lower. As with **Help to Buy**, homes that can be bought using the scheme are limited to new builds and resales by housing associations.

Chapter Seven: The Other Stuff

Record Keeping and Filing: Is incredibly boring but extremely necessary. Thankfully, most of it can now be done digitally and without the need for endless box files. Nonetheless, some will still be needed. Normally, employers, banks and brokers will provide end of year tax information in a form necessary to file tax returns. It is not up to the individual to guess how much they have been paid and how much has been deducted. All of this should go into a paper or digital file marked "TAX". Other necessary files (whether digital or paper) include:

1. Appliances and guarantees.
2. Bank correspondence and bank statements.
3. Car, including car insurance and copy of driving license.

4. Computer and information technology.

5. Council tax and television license (if they still exist).

6. Credit card Statements.

7. Family stuff: birth certificates, letters of wishes from, relatives in case of incapacity, copies of wills, copies of passports, marriage, or divorce documents and so forth.

8. Financial and savings. These may contain sub-folders for ISAs, SIPPs, brokerage accounts, etc.

9. Health insurance, if applicable.

10. Holidays: details of planned and past holidays.

11. Household maintenance (plumbing, central heating service, chimney sweeping, repairs, annual cleaning etc.). In the case of a major renovation project, that should be a separate file.

12. Insurance: household insurance, claims and correspondence.

13. Memberships and subscriptions.

14. Utility bills.

Additionally, a large box for sentimental items will be useful. If there are children, in addition to a lot more filings, several large sentimentality boxes will be needed. Children and pets will also need a separate file for each child or pet. In the case of children, this will grow to several sub-folders for each child.

Consumer Disputes

1. **Prevention:** Prevention is the best course of action. Litigation is both time consuming and emotionally draining. Beware of vague or unclear language in correspondence; needless to say, keep records of all correspondence. It is always better to write a quick return email, setting out understandings and expectations and, most of all the costs involved. Like this:

Dear Mr/Ms. Tigger,
Thank you for taking the time to visit and for your letter dated _____ sent following your visit. A signed copy is enclosed.
I confirm that I would like you to proceed with the replacement of the two windows in the upstairs bedroom, as discussed in my meeting with Mr Piglet on _____, at a total cost of £___. As requested, I have transferred £___ to your account as part payment; please confirm receipt. ***Time is at rather a premium in this project and accordingly, we are anticipating that the windows will be installed and functioning***

within two months from the date of this letter, as I discussed with your representative on the telephone.

I understand that your workmen will deliver, assemble, and install the windows in a competent and workmanlike manner without damage to the surrounding decoration and that in the course of your home survey you have determined that such installation is practicable and feasible. I would be grateful if you would send me a copy of whatever preparatory instructions you feel we ought to have at your earliest convenience. I would also be grateful if you would clarify the nature and extent of any guarantees and warranties.
Yours sincerely,
Eeyore (Ms)

The paragraph in bold, above, makes time of the essence. (Obviously don't leave it in bold in the letter.). Without a "time of the essence" provision, the counterparty can say that a failure to complete the project on time is not a violation of the contract. At some point, a court would have to agree that there was a failure to perform, but it could take a very long time.

2. **Cure:** If you are not happy with the work done, goods supplied or service provided, a phone

call or email to the company may be sufficient. Take photos of everything possible, as seems to be expected in these days of smartphones. If payment was made through a credit card company or PayPal, call them; they may be able to sort the problem out without much further involvement on the part of the consumer. Complaints can also be made to the local Trading Standards department, although they tend to be overwhelmed and therefore not very interested in individual complaints. If those strategies are not effective, then two, possibly three, letters need to be written before recourse to legal action. The first is a letter of complaint which sets out:

1. The contract, which might not be in writing. As a matter of law, whatever you paid for (whether a service or good) should be fit for the purpose for which it was intended and not faulty. This is automatically part of the sale of goods or services, even without any written contract.
2. What went wrong
3. Any relevant legislation (like the Consumer Rights Act 2015), codes of conduct, industry standards, etc. For example, there are several rules governing the behaviour of landlords regarding rental property.

4. The problem, damage caused (delays, money lost, cost of remedy, physical damage to a person or property), and why you are in the right.

5. The desired remedy (money, replacement, etc.).

6. The fact that you are sure this is not the way that they usually do business and that they will no doubt be anxious to help.

Add as many photos and other bits of evidence as possible so their absence cannot be used as an excuse for a delay in resolving the problem. At this point, it may be useful to quote the Consumer Rights Act 2015 if the requisite standard has not been met. The act states that goods must be fit for the purpose for which they are intended and that services must be performed with reasonable care and skill. If you are dealing with a company in a regulated industry, consider copying the regulator.

3. **Regulators:** Assuming an unsatisfactory response or no response, in the case of a regulated industry, appeal to the regulator or ombudsmen. The regulator may be able to help without the need for further action. Regulated services and industries include: banking and insurance, utilities, airlines, the medical and legal professions, and many others. Financial services companies are regulated

by the Financial Conduct Authority, the mention of which does seem to have a terrifying effect.

4. **Twitter (and other social media platforms):** Tweeting dissatisfaction is always an option and can be very effective. Do take care, however, not to exaggerate or say anything that is not entirely true to avoid a libel claim or counterclaim.

5. **Legal Advice, Small Claims Court and Action:** If there is no regulator, then a second letter will be necessary and should contain a threat of legal action within 14 days. Cases involving large sums of money will need proper legal advice from a qualified solicitor. For smaller matters, free advice is available from the Citizens Advice Bureau and, as always, the internet. There are also several free advice websites, depending on the situation. For a small fee, the Small Claims Court will deal with matters worth up to £5,000, at the time of writing. The claim can be filed online and the instructions are simple to follow, following the format of the first letter of complaint. The only problem with the Small Claims Court is that there is no appeals process and the judges are not very experienced and sometimes come to cases with their own prejudices and views. Mostly, however, it is very effective. The letter before recourse to the Small Claims Court should go to the company's registered office by form of delivery requiring a signature, allowing 14

days for a response. The registered office is usually at the bottom of any formal correspondence and can easily be found on the Companies House website.

To: Totally Incompetent Developers Limited
At registered Office
<u>By recorded delivery</u>
DATE
Dear [Firm Name],
Re: Building Works at_____
I understand that you are the owners of ____. I am the owner of one of the immediately neighbouring properties, _____. I am writing to you about the damage done to my property because of the negligence or deliberate actions of your contractor. As you will see from the enclosed letter, I have already tried to communicate with them about this matter; unfortunately, I have had no response.

The cause of the problem was a large tree on your property which had been staked to the wall behind my house. On _____, without notice or consultation, your builders detached this tree from the wall in order to demolish the wall. The obvious and clearly foreseeable result (see photos) was that the tree did fall into my garden, very badly, where it killed two of my trees and might easily have killed or injured a person or animal in the way at the time. Your Project Manager was extremely uncooperative (as he has been throughout this process) and initially claimed it was the wind. When we eventually managed to show the builders on site that this was not the case, it took over a week of repeated phone calls to get them to clean up the mess they had made.

As a result of these actions:

1. I have spent an enormous amount of time, as well as money, dealing with this.

2. I have lost two trees.

3. I had to get a specialist gardener to come and finish the job (see attached invoice A).

4. I will need to replace the trees which will also be very expensive (see attached invoice B).

I have enclosed photographs of the garden before, during and after this disaster, together with copies of the bill and estimates from the gardener. I would be grateful if you would forward to me a cheque for the amount of £___ within the next 14 days to compensate me and to resolve this matter. If I do not receive a satisfactory response from you within 14 days of the date of this letter, I intend to issue proceedings against you in court without further notice. I look forward to your acknowledgement of this letter.

Yours sincerely,

Really very cross indeed (Ms)
Enclosures

Insurance

Insurance contracts should be read with great care and with scrutiny, even. The number of exceptions is extraordinary. The consumer advice columns of the broadsheet newspapers are filled with very sad stories about people who paid all their premiums in good faith, only to have a claim denied on a technicality. Most recently, there was the incredibly sad case of a widow denied payment on her husband's life insurance policy. The policy required him to have his blood pressure tested annually by a doctor or nurse at his GP, another surgery, or a hospital. During lockdown, this was very difficult (if not impossible), so the man duly went to the trouble of having his blood pressure tested by the local chemist. He then died, not because of an incorrect or negligent reading, and the policy refused to pay out to the widow (after many years of paying premiums) because of the technicality. This is how these companies make their money.

What could the couple have done differently? Well, most insurance companies operate telephone helplines. If the man had phoned to explain what he was doing and the company had agreed, they would have been "estopped" from denying the claim. Still, not something which would have occurred to most people under the circumstances. The moral of the story (other than that the company in this case had no morals), is to read the policy carefully, take note of the exclusions and ask for clarification if anything is unclear. For example, most property policies exclude damage due to terrorism, even though that damage would likely be catastrophic for the homeowner. Most travel insurance policies have limits on dangerous sports, as do many life insurance policies. During the most recent lockdown, many businesses discovered, too late, that they were unclear about whether they were covered for the subsequent losses by their business continuity insurance. Always ask, take notes and names, and ask whether the conversation is recorded.

Do not commit amateur revenge; it backfires

Revenge may be a dish served with ice cold vodka and ice cream on the side, but it is also dangerous. Needless to say, physical violence is completely unacceptable and property damage is highly risky, not to mention illegal. Posting intimate photos of former lovers online is also illegal. The problem with revenge is that it can completely undermine any later legal action. Better to go with the steps outlined above. Legally sanctioned revenge is a different matter. It would only be one's patriotic duty to mention someone's tax evasion to the authorities. Or to let the police know about a drinking and driving problem.

Online reviews (as long as they are truthful) on Trust Pilot or TripAdvisor can also be very satisfying.

In the case of a personal matter, there is always a "revenge body". But get fabulous, think of Karma and be done. A restraining order is not a good look.

The worst problems involve neighbours; usually noise, gardens, and animals. A separate book could be written about overhanging trees and another about pervy or exhibitionist neighbours (there are almost certainly several books available on the subject). The police and the council are usually reluctant to intervene. Be very careful before buying a property about whether the reason the vendors are selling is to get away from impossible neighbours. It should be on the vendor's questionnaire.

Write a Will

Anyone with any assets to speak of should consider writing a will. A very simple form of will is available at most stationers; many charities will also help with writing a will in the hope that a legacy will be left to them (although they do not give legal advice). Dying without a will means that the assets pass under the law of intestate succession to whoever is deemed appropriate by the state. In the case of an unmarried, childless person, this would be the parents in the first instance, then various other relations if the parents have predeceased the individual. So, in the case of wealthy parents who do not need the money, it might be preferable to leave the assets to a more needy relation or even a charity. Marriage automatically revokes all previous wills, and a new will should be made at that point. It is worth repeating that cohabiting individuals have no automatic rights of inheritance. A new will needs to be made upon the birth of children, as most people with limited assets would not wish to disinherit a spouse in favour of small children.

Hopefully, the will should not be needed for many years and certainly not because of death arising out of amateur revenge gone wrong.